<u>Don't Tell the Children</u>

Written by

Alexandra Walker

Story by

Alexandra Walker & Stanley Swindling

First paperback edition May 2024

ISBN 979-8-8693-4136-5 (paperback)

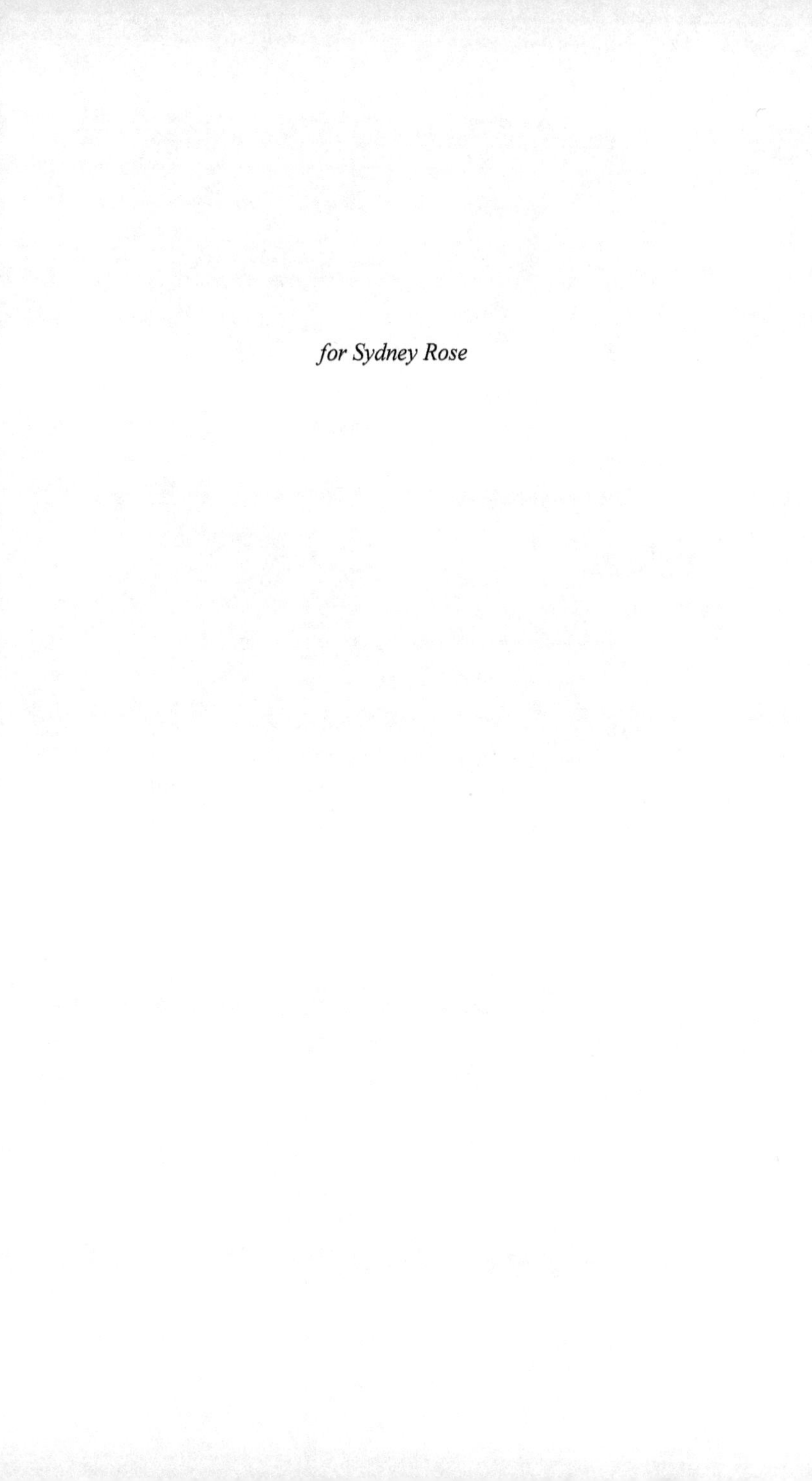

for Sydney Rose

Seraphina

from her journal

In the darkness, on my knees, the great cathedral organ shakes me by my bones, dancing blood inside my ears, so there is no sound but God. In the church, in my Ascension dress, on my Ascension Day, with my Ascension blindfold tight across my eyes, there is no sight but God. In the silence, my breath is needles, my ribs are promised, my mouth is crime, yet there is no touch but God. But there in the darkness, there in the church, there, before the silence came, I found something. I don't think I was meant to. I think I was meant to be afraid. I think we all were meant to be afraid. But it was like some kind of taste, someplace deep inside, that I had never known. And I liked it. I liked this place I could not reach. I liked this place where magic lived. Where it prickled. Where it spilled over. And I heard it say to me that I was magic, I was power. Power, itself. It was an accident. Fumbling like an infant in a crib, I felt guilt. I had shame. For a moment only. It was when High Father sang out through the deep silence thanking God for us, the strong crop of the faithful. But I think I was told to feel shame once. I think it was my mother, or my father, or even the High Father himself. And then my friend returned. My warm, my magic, my power, my new power. Perhaps God lives within me now. He drinks tea between my clavicles. He bathes beneath my aorta. Perhaps He lives in all of us. Perhaps that is what Ascension Day is really for. For letting in the magic. But when High Father said the words, we all undid our blindfolds, in perfect unison, and I remember this was practiced. This was show. This was theater. Ascension Day is a trick. The magic within is not High Father. It's not even God. This newness is mine alone. And the thrill shocks through across my skin, sparkling inside my gums. I smile as I say amen at the end of the prayer. In perfect unison with forty-eight other newly ascended children, just as we rehearsed. My eyes float up and land on the sad, sad expression of our poor, lamenting Christ Jesus. Glowing dreadfully in his stained glass. I don't understand it then, nor now, but my eyes became warm with pricking tears. Forty-eight children rose in unison when beckoned by their standing parents, and I followed quickly after, missing the cue altogether to ascend from adolescence into blisteringly bright adulthood. And the shame paints my cheeks hot red. Across the aisle I see him turn to look at me. He isn't supposed to. And for that my chest tingles. Harley has always loved me. I think he always will.

Harley

from his journal

My father, and the Council of Leaders, I suppose, have advised me to begin an account, to track daily proceedings, and to reflect on spiritual changes, now that I am a man. This will not be official record, but personal dictation, for my benefit. I will try to maintain regular entries beginning now.

Today was my Ascension Day. It was magnificent. It was more powerful than I ever expected. To have gone in a boy and come out a man was fulfilling. Father's sermon was very moving. I especially liked when he compared God undoing our blinding sin and returning us to Eden as we undid the blindfolds.

We are so fortunate to be exalted children of a loving and magnanimous God, who sought pity on our wretched souls, who saw light beneath the filth of our crimes against Him for so long. We live in peace and prosperity deep within the earth He created for us, the very same one we destroyed with the poisons of our wars and perversions.

We may never return to the surface, but I don't think I want to. The air is toxic, the water is venom, and the soil is ash, thus, it is said, only demons could thrive in such a place. Here the air is cool and soft, the water is clean and sweet, the food is bountiful. Our Holy Garden is safe, and remains safe because our souls are clean, and because our High Father guides us righteously.

It is an honor to be the son of the High Father. And yet it █████████ ███████████████████████ weight that I █████████████ █████████████ great shame. [1]

I am not perfect, just as no one is. Our lives are monuments to our endless endeavors for perfection. I confess I let my heart be distracted for a moment during the ceremony today, and it brings me a small disappointment in myself to be distracted from the light of God. Although it was no crime, as it was my betrothed who caught my eye. Sera was out of step with us as we ascended, and our eyes met.

I admit she has always been unique. I admit freely that this is what makes me love her. God has great purpose for her, I believe, for she carries within her a strong passion.

After the ascension was complete, and we were in the reception gala, we found each other. She looked magnificent today, as did everyone in their finest Ascension Day regalia of fitted black suits and lovely white

---

[1] This section appears to have been scratched out. What remains is what could be discerned through the redactions.

dresses.

Seraphina though, as is so typical of her, was an outlier. She had these dark red trims and laces throughout her white dress. It wasn't much, but I knew she picked it to make a point, to say that none of us could be pure as pure is pure. She's smart, and funny like this. She's a Scholar track, so she reads and studies everything we have, and knows more about God than I think any of us could. We're going to be on the Council of Leaders when the time comes. We smiled whenever someone noticed her red fabrics and jewels. She knows it's because they are startled, but I told her it was because she was beautiful, and beauty can be regarded as beautiful. It isn't a lie after all, she is beautiful. Her dark hair and her dark eyes made the reds so vibrant.

Anyway, I think I may be misunderstanding the point of this journal. I'm not sure what is pertinent to record. I'll continue.

At the reception, we fielded several questions from parents and friends alike, all wondering when we were to be married as we are now of age. We handled it well, but I wonder if everyone is asked these things, since our class is anywhere from 17 to 19, surely some of us aren't ready for marriage.

In fact, I know some of us are not even betrothed yet. Byrn Chamberley, for instance, isn't even steady with anyone, despite his charm and beauty and popularity. Many people went up to him after, plenty of girls in our class, and he was always friendly.

And he was handsome today too. He had rolled his sleeves up after the ceremony was over, which should have looked messy, but didn't. I think it must be an athlete thing, because his muscles are bigger than mine so his jacket must fit tighter, so it was probably more comfortable. He had combed his blonde hair in this way that must have been solely for his parents' benefit because they kept fixing it whenever he messed it up. He is a mystery to me, how someone so golden seems to be so alone.

When he caught me watching him, which I now think should have been embarrassing but somehow wasn't, he seemed to smile in this way that meant we knew something no one else did, except I have no idea what it could be. When I tried to smile back, I couldn't. I just watched him smiling at me. But then I did feel embarrassed, so I looked away and returned to the conversations with our friends and parents like it was nothing at all. It was a curious thing, and he is a curiosity, and I think I will pray on that further.

But the rest of the reception was nice. The grand ballroom was decorated beautifully. Everyone's speeches were charming. Elysa gave a very inspiring speech about our futures, and our past, and how God is within all of it, as we will be within each other's lives always, and she even started to cry, as did a lot of the women, but not Sera. I think despite Sera and Elysa being best friends, there is a sort of tension between them. I sometimes sense it, when they disagree, but that is not often, and their love is always much truer than any conflicts. I am sure she will be the godmother to our children.

Then we danced, hand in hand, arm in arm, slowly and politely, and quite beautifully. I caught my father smiling as he watched us dance to the soft quartet. It filled me with pride, to know he saw me and felt satisfaction in me as his son.

After, when I walked Seraphina to her room, we paused a moment to talk. And in the glow of the evening floor lights, she looked at me so strangely, like she was in a pain of some kind, waiting to tell me of something that troubled her.

We were alone there, and I confess I did kiss her. We have only kissed outside of wedlock 4 times now. I am ashamed of my flesh, again distracting my heart from focusing on God. My excitement for her is strong, and I think it is only so because my love for her is so deep.

For a moment, only a moment, we were more than a strict kiss though. We were hands on skin as well. She pressed herself to me. She made a sound. It was something quiet and delicate, and it broke me for only a moment. I was dizzy from it all. And I quickly stopped us from committing a regretful mistake. I pulled away.

Her eyes were closed, and she apologized, but I was not angry. I smiled and I touched her cheek and told her goodnight. I am pleased to be so loved by God that I know He is not angry with me. Our love is no crime, and when we are married, we will be joined in His holy light.

After, I returned to my quarters, and wrote this entry. I'm not sure how to end this, so I just will. I am tired and will go to sleep now.

Seraphina

a schedule she kept as a bookmark

7:05am – 7:50am	Breakfast
7:55am – 8:35am	Communal Prayer/Service/Announcements
8:40am – 9:25am	Corporeal Study
9:30am – 10:15am	Prophets, Saints, and Persecution
10:20am – 11:05am	Origination of Sins
11:10am – 11:55am	Physical Education
12:00pm – 12:50pm	Lunch
1:05pm – 1:28pm	Current and Non-Canon Scripture
1:28pm – 1:50pm	Scripture Exegesis
1:55pm – 2:18pm	Spiritual Interpretation
2:18pm – 2:40pm	Language Translation
2:45pm – 3:15pm	Communal Study
3:30pm – 5:00pm	Rehearsal

written on the back of her schedule [2]

He kissed me again. I cannot lift my carcass from the pool. I am gone again. And again. He is the clash of sounds in a play. He begins quietly. He crescendos and then I am cold. His song always ends before the morning. Before the night, even. I feel the lights dim beneath my hair. It is always now. In Corporeal they demonstrated God's perfect union. Professor and her husband. Wrapped in plain garments. A kiss, maybe, she said. The lights were all on. He enters her and she explains. Telling us what God loves. But I am gone again. My magic is spinning someplace far down. She has become him. Her husband is me. We are strange though. Coiling sea monsters. The last ones left. Desperate. It is different. Ours is different. And I know they are wrong for it. Somehow. I am the High Father, and I am shining.

---

[2] This entry is included due to its interpretation of proceeding Harley's record of their kiss after Ascension Day. The reference to the live, in-class sex demonstration in Corporeal Studies is believed to only occur after Ascension Day.

Harley

from his journal

Tonight I went to the theater to see Seraphina and the rest of our senior class perform the triannual play. Scholar tracks are always so fascinating to me. The Horticulture track is never so exciting. Nearly the entire community was present this evening.

Father and mother sat in the box seats along with others from the Council of Leaders. After discussion, I was able to convince him to let me sit with my peers in the floor seats near the stage. It is better to be among them if I am to lead them. I also admit it's more fun, and I suppose I wanted to better see Seraphina perform.

She had seemed strange after her class did the Appropriate Corporeal Union Presentation. I thought it may have unsettled her. Some Council Leaders have proposed revising the Corporeal Studies curriculum for women, as they are the more sensitive sex, but when I asked Sera about it, she seemed angry with me for suggesting so. I dropped it after that, and now believe she was simply nervous about her first performance. She was playing Saint Ashli herself in The Final Days of Saint Ashli, which must be a big responsibility. When I saw her after the show, she seemed energized again, so that must have been it.

Before I go on and marvel at the wonderful production, I feel it is necessary to document an interesting occurrence tonight. As it would seem, God has encouraged my curiosity surrounding my classmate, Byrn Chamberley.

Tonight, as everyone made their way down the flights of stairs to the theater's level, I felt compelled to look up the center. I thought at first that I was just curious to see so many people making their way down the spiral of stairs all at once, yet when I looked up, I only found Byrn. He was a few flights above and looking down, directly at me. When our eyes met, I froze, and I think he froze too. We seemed to just be watching one another.

Maybe he was just curious too, and wanted to look down the spiral, but I don't think so because he smiled at me. And again, when he smiled at me, he seemed to be knowing something about us. I only nodded, I think, but I did try to smile back this time, even though I don't think I actually did smile.

That was the first event. The second was when we were in the theater, and I was in my seat. My mind wandered as I waited, and I reflected on the strange coincidence of Byrn looking down at the same time I was compelled to look up. As I was wondering what it meant, I turned around without thinking. I thought then that I was just looking around at everyone filling the ornate performance space with their beautiful evening wear, yet, again, there was Byrn. He was walking down the aisle, and our eyes met. His eyes are blue.

I believe Byrn and I may be destined to form some connection, as a feeling swelled within my chest, and I suddenly hoped his seat was next to mine.

It wasn't, although he did sit close, which I found relieving. He was in the row directly in front of mine, and two seats to my right. Before he sat down, he smiled at me again, and said hello. I felt foolish for a moment, because I had been watching him the whole time, and in my embarrassment I didn't say anything back. Although I did smile this time.

He did not talk to me again after that. He was chatting with Tessianne, who was sitting next to him. I'm not sure if they came together, or if they just happened to be sitting next to each other. Because I was originally sitting with father, I didn't get to pick seats with my friends, and was therefore sat between two gentlemen who I knew only remotely, and who were more interested in their dates. I found myself paying more and more attention to Byrn and Tessianne, although I could not hear their conversation over the ambient chatter, I wished to be part of it.

Perhaps he sensed as much, for there was a lull in their conversation shortly before the play began, and he turned his head to look at me. I panicked and looked away at first, but then looked back at him because he was, after all, turning and looking directly at me. He didn't say anything though, just nodded.

Then the lights dimmed, and the play began, and he watched the play. Although before I go on to describe the play, I should remark on what happened along the way. This all seems evident for some plan God seems to have for Byrn and myself.

During the play, although we were not together, sitting beside one another, it felt at times that we were watching it together, communicating without words. When I would laugh, he would laugh, almost in agreement. If I gasped, he would similarly respond soon after. I would listen for his reaction and watch the silver curve where the stage lights would outline the side of his head, and his ear, and his neck, and his shoulder. At one point even, I think he almost turned to look back. But that could have been something else.

At the end, I felt a swell again, because I knew he was crying, and I'd never seen a ███ man like him cry.

Which is the end of my notes on the interaction with Byrn.

The play itself was fantastic. The Holy Spirit moved through us all, I believe, as we watched the performance. Although I am not a Scholar track, I will try my best to explain what we saw.

The lights around us had all gone dark, and the stage lights would glow and change color as the story progressed. The Final Days of Saint

Ashli begins with the proclamation of the coming apocalypse. The fools try to fight, and the chosen ones brilliantly build the Holy Garden into the earth, as was directed by God through the dictation from Saint Kyle. These early scenes were bright.

Then the play becomes darker and redder as the wars and riots grew closer, and the rejected sinners grew desperate. The orchestra was loud and played very deep sounds during these scenes. Our forefathers completed construction of the New Eden, and rejoiced, which was bright and happy. Saint Ashli tried to bring peace to the violent sinners whom God would not allow into His New Eden. The soldiers of Caesar errantly believed they could force God's exalted children to break covenant and poison His Holy Garden with sinners and demons. Saint Ashli reasoned and pleaded, and I choked up as Seraphina fell to her knees and begged God to keep them away.

In the end, Saint Ashli went out into the chaos, and God transformed her into a weapon of light, 7 million spears, and holy fire, exploding her outward, erasing the soldiers, sinners, and demons as they all tried to force their way into our Holy Garden. On stage, the characters who were the bad ones held these tubes that shot sparks out of the end, because the soldiers tried shooting guns to win. The music climaxed and Seraphina became God's holy weapon by way of a bright light and this mechanism which grew out from behind her. It was like several gold wings and spears grew from her back and spread out. A glowing crown of daggers did similarly from behind her head. It was spectacular and we all gasped at its beauty. The bad ones all fell and threw confetti and ribbons into the air because Saint Ashli made them all into ash and pieces with God's wrath.

Then a choir of angels sang as they lifted Seraphina with wires up into the ceiling to show that Saint Ashli rose to heaven. Then the curtain fell, and everyone applauded and cheered. When Sera came out to bow, Byrn stood up just before I did to clap for her. I yelled and clapped so hard my hands hurt. It was incredible how amazing she was. Her dictation was moving. I felt proud to be her betrothed. When her eyes found me in the crowd, she smiled at me in that strange way that she sometimes does.

Then I saw something change in her face. It wasn't quite like she looks when she is angry, but it seemed like something distracted her, almost like she was confused. When I tried asking her about it after, she didn't know what I meant. Being a performer in front of so many people must be so overwhelming, I cannot imagine it. She must be feeling so many things, and so all I did was congratulate her, and comfort her, and celebrate her.

She couldn't sleep so we went to the forest room. It was so late, so almost no one was there. We talked, and she told me about everything backstage. I admit she was so beautiful and spectacular, beneath the twinkling lights in the ceiling, surrounded by the replica trees and forest soundtrack, it was so peaceful and beautiful that I nearly kissed her again, but I did not. Instead, I suggested we pray, and thank God for such a wonderful night and performance.

When I finished saying the prayer, I said amen, and opened my eyes, and saw that she was lying there, silently, with her eyes open, watching the twinkling lights in the dark ceiling above. I laid beside her and held her hand.

We were in such a quiet peace, and yet I felt like I was Saint Ashli, that I could explode into fire and spears at any moment. We just laid there without talking. But I could hear her breathing become quicker and louder. With my hand in hers, she lifted it to her face and touched it to her cheek and her mouth. I closed my eyes and held my breath, and the warmth of God filled me, and I knew I had to obey Him.

She asked me what I was thinking about, but I was not thinking about anything. I could only think about the softness of her cheek, and her breath upon my hand. I could only think of the fragile noise she had made when we kissed last.

I said I was thinking of nothing, and she told me she always felt overcome by thought. She started to say something that she didn't finish, she said, "I think that I…" and then said nothing. When I urged her to continue, she didn't.

Then she asked me to walk her back to her room and I did. It hurt, in a way, when I said good night and did not kiss her. It hurt deeply everywhere when I did not hold her. It hurt like a hunger hurts, except it was in my arms, and my mouth, and my chest, and elsewhere. But I know my spirit has grown stronger because of this. My father would be proud.

This evening has been incredible, and I will never forget it, but now I will go to sleep, because I am so tired. Good night.

Alexandra Walker

Seraphina

from her journal

We have no more saints left. We are at an empty table, and everyone is fat and teethy smiles, and 'We have no need for saints now' and I am left wondering who else is hungry. Who else is left to love the spiders underground. I am Saint Ashli for a moment, and it floats me to the water's surface. I wear her words like gowns I cannot fit in. I scream and I beg, and they all stared without anything to say. I am a toddler beyond the wall now, and the dragons are circling above me, and I feel my ankles deep in the ash. I am all shakes and shivers. I become fire and spear and I see their terror. I see their awe. Saint Ashli does not laugh. But Saint Seraphina may. There are no saints. There is only us. There is only me. We twist and we cry, begging them, in the stage lights, but it is all pretend, and their tears are all pretend. I fear I am pretend. I know Saint Ashli. I wore her death like soil and bile. I wore her destruction like a crown. I would be fire and spear unkilled. My destruction would be my destruction, and God would only watch. And my fears have me shiver, and I leave the empty table, writhing with fat, teethy smiles, all gnashing. I am lowered, I am me, I am at the curtain, I am bowed, I am returned. I find him and he finds me. Harley. He is a light in a dark place. I would swallow him if he were poison, and he would wear me if I were colorful thorns. Then a splintering happens. This one is the boy from class. The quiet one who became a tall man. The spiraling pillar, admired, and I see him fill with cracks, small ones, splendid, perfect cracks, they go all the way to the top, I think. He is crying. He does not smile, like all the other fat, teethy smiles. He is undone. He sees me. And I see him. And I do not know how far down he can see of me. And I think that scares me. But Byrn is only the boy from class. And I do not know him. And he will not know me. And I wonder about him in the forest room. I wonder if he hates it there. I wonder if he prays like Harley prays, perfect and rote. I wonder if Saint Ashli wondered as I do. About her loves when she was a fury of God. I wonder if she had loves. As I do. Or if they feared her, as I fear me, and as Harley, surely, would fear me. I am a fear of Eden. The only Saint left. And my blood is ice. And God must know, I think. If he wants my blood hot. He will have to burn me. And I wonder, then, who will watch. And who will hold my burning hands.

Harley

from his journal

My father has bestowed upon me a great honor today. I am officially a junior council member. The title itself comes with no honors or esteem, although I am permitted into some inner workings of leadership. I am permitted behind the curtain, so to speak, to observe and grow, so that I may be shaped into an adequate Council Leader when the time comes. Father has explained that this will come with responsibility, and expectation, as I finish out my Horticulture track. I expect I may one day guide the Council of Sustenance, even if father hopes to pass the title of High Father to me, that is not his choice alone. I am proud to work with him anyhow.

I am to sit with him for periods, while he works, and be tutored in high knowledge. I am also to join him for social meetings with council members and premier patricians. Tonight was my first of such meetings, a dinner with the Helleck matriarch, whom I only know as Madame Helleck, and her sons, Paul and Phillip.

Although I understand fully the importance of the work father does, as well as the whole of the Council of Leaders, I find the work of social meetings very dry, and tedious. It was business, of course, under the guise of pleasure, where even the consumption of the food felt calculated. The conversation, the real one, between the polite prefaces of vague interest in hobbies, felt so dull and unimportant. We discussed and conjectured and queried to no real resolution over concerns Madame Helleck invented.

Her lights were too dim, though hers were brightest.

Her quarters were too warm, though her suite had the most cooling vents.

She wanted assurance her rationing would be lightest. A thing father later described as "a fixed amount during a shortage," which he of course promised her she would have because never has New Eden had shortage and never would it. It was such an empty and boring thing he could grant everyone. The Councils of Community and Sustenance work in seamless efficiency to create far more than the entire community would need 10 times over.

She even felt choice marriage unions were not sufficient, and argued for arrangements, despite both her sons already being married, and it all █████████████████████████████████

It just seemed so hard to comprehend the value of, as none of the things we discussed are things anyone is ever in want of. Our Eden has plenty of power, always, food, always, unions of choice, always. Our Eden is a place of abundance and surplus, and so the shuffling and bartering for it, for more of it, felt so superfluous and so small.

But when I asked father about it, he assured me it was all the game, all the system, all the workings, all the plan as God intended. He explained further, at home, when I failed to grasp his meaning. He said, "It is the way of man to want more. Our purpose is to love God, and to love God is to love His heavenly perfection, and to desire for it. On earth, we cannot ever have such a thing, and so it is our function to want more. Here, in His Holy Garden, where all our needs are met, and more, we, the holy Council of Leaders, must guide the wanting."

I ███████████████████████████████████████
██
████████ wanting is not love ████████████████
██
████ the surface, wanting ███████████████████
██
██
███████████████████ I just [3]

It is best for me to sleep now. To pray on this further, and then sleep. I am unsettled for some reason. I believe I am overtired.

---

[3] He has stopped mid-sentence and scratched out heavily here. What remains is what could be discerned.

Seraphina

written in the margins of Genesis Chapter 1,
torn from a Bible, and later stored in her journal [4]

I have read about sunrises. I know they are slow. The planet turns and up they come, and the sky fills with hot light from a violent ball of plasma millions of miles away. It is a cruel relentless thing, incessant, and painful. If I could be millions and millions and millions of miles away it would not be far enough. I am endangered by my own self. She is a thing in a mirror, betraying me, enthralling me. She cuts herself into morsels and feeds me and yet I am consumed by it. It happened in gym class. He is new to me now. When he was once wallpaper and white noise, he has become a thing I see, a smell I awaken for, a verse that I can't recall memorizing, yet speak freely. I have always had gym class with Byrn. I saw today, for the first time, that I have always had gym class with Byrn. I am a girl again. I turn to find him. I seek him in the crowd of male heads. I observe him. I observe him. I observe him. I observe him. And when he sees he only looks. I am shy without control. I am a girl again. We are women running in a circle. We are women crunching abdominals. We are women pushing our weight up from the ground with only our arms and I am sweating and I am watching him. Because he is a man, like all the others, lifting weights, climbing ropes, pulling himself up at a bar, repeatedly, repeatedly, and he doesn't have his shirt on anymore because it is hot in the gym and he has taken his off. It is hanging on his shoulder and his shoulder is big. And I see his back. And his back shines with sweat. And I am all the beasts that walk the earth and have no soul. His back ripples and flexes with taut muscle beneath skin. I would open him. I would dismantle him. I would nest my body there and hide beneath his covers. It is a sunrise in me. Slow and hot and bright. It replaces me. And when he finishes, he lands on his feet, and he finds me, and I am staring, pushing myself up over and over, dripping, wet hair dangling, threatening him with eyes of tart lust. And I see him. His chest, thick, rise and fall, rise and fall, thirsty for oxygen. His jaw clenches. Body heavy. Eyes on mine. He threatens me back. And I fear that I am gone again.

---

[4] Because Scholar tracks would have had multiple personal holy texts to study and notate in freely, the theories surrounding the significance of Seraphina ripping a page from her King James Bible are mostly moot. Rather than a defiant choice, the use of the page was likely one of hasty convenience, as it was found folded and stored chronologically in her private journal, which she presumably did not have available to her during the school day.

Seraphina

from her journal

I ruin everything. I ruin everything. I am [5]

---

[5] This partial entry ends here, and is included due to its likely significance in context to Harley's following entry.

Harley

from his journal

She came to me today, my darling Seraphina. My soul has been perplexed and aching under the pressures of new responsibility, and she was like a medicine.

I was in the tropical wing of the greenhouse level, along with the rest of my class in Floral Propagation III. She came in tenderly, and very quietly, though she was so troubled, I could see she was, by her eyes and her breath. She was like Eve in the First Garden of Eden, brought to me by God, shaded and shrouded with foliage, watching me, waiting for me.

My heart felt like it had melted and flooded my entire chest and throat in a tingling warmness and I snuck away to be with her. We were alone behind glistening fronds and colorful petals, slick with the soft mist that floated here. She looked ethereal, like a dream.

She buried herself into my chest, sighing as though she were relieved. She held me and I asked if she was okay but for a while she didn't answer me. When she did finally pull away from my chest, she looked up, and she kissed me.

It shocked me to my stomach and numbed everything else. She kissed and kissed and kissed for so long, and I could only bathe in it. Her lips were wet and smooth, and they cushioned against mine like something holy. She moved and pressed like some kind of dance that I could not keep up with. I felt her tongue and my head went dizzy. She was in my mouth, and I remember feeling afraid, but feeling a new thing as well, like the fear was a good thing, and I wanted more of it. I grabbed her, and gripped her, and I think it was around her ribs, and I pressed against her.

But I pressed too far, and we collided with the racks of ferns and other plants and they rattled and my mind snapped back into me. We separated and, in fear, the cold kind that isn't good, I pulled her away, further back into the greenhouse, away from my classmates.

When we stopped, we just stared at each other for a moment, hesitating, knowing what is forbidden, wondering if it's alright, and I think waiting for the other one to decide for us both. We were breathing heavily, and my skin felt hot. Eventually she swallowed and seemed to compose herself, standing up a little straighter. She said my name, and I said hers. Then she started to cry. Not full on, just sort of teared up, and then wiped her eyes.

She told me she killed a spider. She said it was an accident, and that she loved it. She told me it was a thing she found, and that she cared for it. But it died. And I tried to comfort her and reassure her, but she insisted it was her fault. She said it was in a jar, so it was safe, and she had given it air holes, and would sing to it. She kept saying she loved it, that it was special, and that it had found her. She said God had brought this spider to her, to be good to, because spiders are God's creatures, even though nobody likes them. She said she loved it, like she had to convince me, and I said I believed her.

She said it died because she loved it all wrong. The tears in her eyes became stronger and she cried, and I held her. She said she kept it, like a pet thing, and that it starved and died because of her, because her love couldn't feed it.

She said it died because a love cannot be a possession, and I tried to tell her it was okay, that we are not possessions, but she was so afraid of killing me. I laughed, and said she wasn't killing me. But she said I wouldn't know it, neither of us would. So we had to promise never to possess each other. I said, "Okay," but she said we needed to say it.

So I said, "Seraphina Caldwell, I promise, before God, never to possess you, and only to love you."

Then she smiled and said, "Harley Valton, I promise, before God, never to possess you, and only to love you." And her face became filled with light and joy and relief and we kissed again. It was sweeter than before. It was lovelier.

And I don't even regret a moment of it, because it was a kiss about a promise, and it was a promise before God, and I think God knows our hearts, and knows our love, and loves our love, and so He must love our kisses too, our promise kisses and our other kisses, because our kisses are our love, all of them, every time, every single time.

So I am content tonight, and I will sleep, and I will ask God to let me dream of her.

Seraphina

from her journal

I am awoken from a nightmare. It is still night. It is still haunting me. Harley was there. We were worried about a pregnancy. I was supposed to be pregnant, but I wasn't. Something was wrong with the baby but the doctor would not tell me what. Byrn was the doctor, and he left because he was busy. Then we were home. But home was in the dining hall, and there were babies in highchairs everywhere, they were in the kitchen, even. And Harley kept saying I needed to feed them because they were hungry and crying. But the highchairs were too high, they were higher than I could reach. And I tried reaching them but I couldn't, and then my teeth were breaking, and I was trying to cough them out. And he said it was because I had lost the baby. And then a baby fell out of its highchair, and it smashed onto the ground, and no one saw it, and I was trying to clean it up with napkins before anyone saw because it wasn't mine. And it was just pink soup, not blood, just pink slop that wouldn't clean up. And my mother came in and told me to hurry because I was late. That we could clean up the baby later. But I had to go to the cathedral. I was supposed to marry Harley an hour ago, she kept saying it over and over. I had dead baby all over my clothes and my hands but I went to the cathedral anyway. And when I arrived everyone was stiff. They moved like puppets, or broken animatronics. They would turn, and kiss, and turn away. They would hump, and their heads would spin, and then they would hump again. They would stab each other, stab, pull out, stab. The High Father crawled on all fours in a small circle. Harley was waiting for me. I asked him why everyone was acting this way. He asked like what. And I couldn't think of the word, and I kept coughing out broken teeth. I didn't want to keep the dead baby a secret. I didn't want the wedding. I didn't want to be there. I kept asking him to leave with me, but he wouldn't. He said we had to do this. I said he promised me. He said Byrn was waiting for us. That he had prepared a picnic in the forest room. But I was angry because Byrn was the doctor with secrets. I asked Harley if this was Hell. I asked if he knew we were in Hell. I asked like he knew and didn't tell me. And then Byrn was there, and Harley asked him if he knew we were in Hell. I asked him why he has secrets. But he ignored us both and put his hand up my skirt. And I said not here, because I wanted it, but not there. But Harley said no one will notice, and he kissed me. But my teeth kept breaking, so I couldn't kiss because I had to spit out the pieces. And Harley told me to drink this, and he tried squeezing a wet washcloth into my mouth, but my hair kept getting in the way, and getting stuck inside my mouth, and I was very thirsty. Byrn brushed my hair away from my face and held it back, and Harley tried squeezing the water drops into my mouth from the washcloth, but they kept getting everywhere, they kept dripping into my eyes. When I awoke, I found that I was crying. I am tormented always, but I cannot say why.

Harley

from his journal

I am tired and sore, but I would like to write about today as it was Prosperity Day, so a lot happened.

My track presented displays of colorful and exotic flora, which were appreciated by everyone. Seraphina's track presented sermons and lectures, which were very moving, but I think I prefer it when they do the plays.

I wish we could all collaborate on one beautiful presentation. I think I will propose the idea to father. If the Arts track did their symphony and painting with the Engineer track's light and water show, along with Horticulture's and Scholar's presentations, it would be truly spectacular. Even Medicine tracks could display something on man's healthy anatomy, and a model could pose and dance, but they always end up showing slides of microbes and healing rashes.

Anyway, the games portion was very exciting. All of our classes put up someone to participate in a game, and it's the only time our tracks are all together at once, besides lunch and study and church, but even then we aren't really doing something all together like in the games.

It was fun, rooting for our tracks, or our friends. Seraphina's class put her in swimming, and she went against Oliver in my track, but I rooted for her anyway. She came in dead last, and she laughed so loud when she found out she lost. She has a magnetic laugh. I love her so much.

My class put me up for the wrestling games, probably because I'm the biggest, which is a laugh because I'm pretty sure I was smaller than all the other tracks. We wrestled in the gym, and everyone seemed to be crowded in there, excited to see the matches. When I went up to wrestle, I was put against Byrn. I'd thought he was a Medicine track, because all the Chamberleys are, but he was representing Engineering. I think everyone knew how it was going to end just by looking at us, but I wasn't going to turn over so easily.

Something had happened shortly before our match, and it feels important to reflect on it now. Seraphina and Byrn were looking at each other. I don't know why, but it was constant, and it struck something foul inside of me. She had been wanting to watch every Engineering game and presentation and I became jealous because I eventually knew she was curious to see him. Then when I saw him look at her, I knew he was interested in her, and it hurt.

At first it hurt because Seraphina is my love, and I had never been met with feelings of jealousy before. I had this fear that she might find him more appealing and lovely than me. She might, after all, since he is.

But then it hurt because he had been interested in me first, or so I thought. I thought maybe he had been looking at me and saying hello to me because he wanted to be close with me, but now it felt like he had only done so because I was Sera's betrothed, and he was only interested in her and getting closer to her through me.

These were the feelings of the Devil that I had been struck by.

So when I stood before him to wrestle I was filled with a jealous anger. I hated him. I hated that he was smiling at me. I hated that he said my name when he said hello. I hated his hair and his muscles and the veins in his arms. I hated, most, most of all, I hated that he seemed hurt by my coldness. He was kind and I was cold with hate. I said, "whatever," and he was hurt by it.

We had all wrestled in gym class, of course, but he was better. Maybe his Medicine family made him stronger, or maybe Engineer tracks were stronger by labor, I don't know. We lunged and grabbed each other. I tried to stay low, to keep him low. I don't know what I was trying, actually. I think another feeling took over, because I was not thinking much.

We were just bodies, forcing and pushing. Trying to put power over the other. I remember my arms around his legs, and his around my chest. I would have his hips, and he would pull my shoulders. Someone was under someone's armpit, someone had someone's neck, a groin would lift into the other, our hands would lock around each other. I remember he was very firm, he was hard like stone, everywhere. His arms squeezed me, and his back was a solid pillar I couldn't move. His hair was soft. I hated it. I hated his grunting. He has this warm and smooth voice, and his grunts are just the same, and they shouldn't be. I would get around him, and he would breathe heavier, and I hated it. He lifted my whole body, but when he tried to pin me I would get under and out and force him to struggle. I was making him work harder than anyone would have expected. We were two of God's sons wrapped around each other

I think he was going easy on me, now. He sounded like he was letting out impressed laughs. I thought I was getting the better of him. But he was laughing at me. Playing with me. He was wrestling against my body for longer than he needed to. I am filled with these cloudy thoughts again. I thought maybe I was matching him. Maybe everyone could see that Byrn wasn't better than me. But he was, of course.

He pinned me. I hit hard, my back to the mat, and him over me, holding me down. We were both warm, and we were both panting, and we were both sweating. Maybe I had matched him. But he did win.

I remember being sad. I remember being sad that he was better than me in front of Seraphina. I remember I was sad after because I really would have liked being friends with Byrn. He has a friendly smell that I like. I remember he kept looking over at me, and he even hugged me and said I did a good job, but I know I hadn't, and here he was, Byrn Chamberley, the friendliest guy to everyone he met.

And I felt so very un-special.

After that, though, everything went well, and everyone had fun. We didn't keep track of winners because we never

Someone has knocked at my door. I'll conclude here.

Seraphina

from her journal

Who made God? I think it was me. I think we have all made him in our image. I think he is paint. If I make God, then aren't I a god? Are we all gods? I used to feel him. But it was my own hands. I used to hear him. But it was my own voice. Everything made sense, before, because I made it so. I am my own god. I am God, and God is me as well. There are more colors than they would let us see. The lock is undone. I am disobedience, and obedience at once. I know, and I do not know. I am good. I am evil. I am me. I am nothing, and I am everything. And I am very afraid. We held our secret games. We are more prosperous than they know. Prosperity day, and prosperity night. Just us, just the ascended, just the kids, we are such silly things, we still go to school, we are not made yet. They will kill me for it one day. But I have woken up in a pile and I am so alone. They are unfinished words, gasping. It was in the forest room. It was late. We played with the fake fires. We danced through the fake trees. We cried out to fake skies. We tired, and we played our games. An invention, I think. To steel our souls, a challenge. Angels and demons, truths and dares, a game, when faced with the choice to sin in your heart, strengthen it, or fail, but free yourself regardless. From sin. From us. And pious Elysa squalled so piously, but then dissolved like powders in hot milk. So much for piety. And it began. And it was good. We were precious. And shaking. We challenged ourselves to the edge. Touch her here. Kiss him there. Dance like this. Open like that. Tell us about yours. Whisper about these. Now be honest. Did you sin in your heart? Did you lie? We all did. Or maybe only I did. No, she says, there is no sin in my heart when Harley kisses me. No, she says, there is no sin in my heart when I kiss Byrn. No, she says, there is no sin in my heart when Byrn kisses Harley. No. There is no sin in my heart. Only dreams. Only stars. Real ones. Millions and millions and millions and millions of them, far away. Burning catastrophically hot. Everything consumed. The three of us. Stars crashing, exploding each other brilliantly. Into gods. Or dust, maybe. Dust. All mixing together. I would be warm in their dust. I would warm them in mine. If only to have them kiss me again.

Harley

from his journal

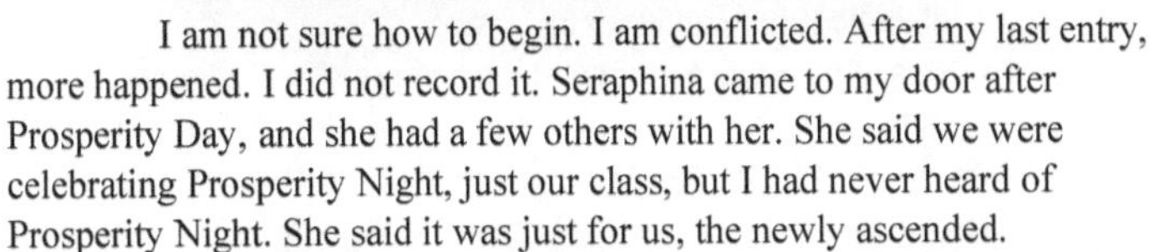

I am not sure how to begin. I am conflicted. After my last entry, more happened. I did not record it. Seraphina came to my door after Prosperity Day, and she had a few others with her. She said we were celebrating Prosperity Night, just our class, but I had never heard of Prosperity Night. She said it was just for us, the newly ascended.

I was going to ask permission from father, since it was now late and I was going to be shadowing him tomorrow, but she said we didn't need permission, and that we should be quiet so as to not wake the parents.

I was nervous, and I was excited, and I slipped out with her and all the others I had seen and known my whole life. It was odd in a way. Here we all were, faces from childhood, matured in ways, dewy and frayed from the day, some of us close and familiar, others only distantly so. Yet here we all were, together, and the same, in a way, because we were complicit, all of us, in a secret. I don't think I thought of it as a secret at first, or maybe I did. I just thought how fun. To be part of an all, to be part of an us, a we. I think I knew, in a way, that I was making an excuse. I was convinced this was the behavior of their future Council Leader, as though to say, I know you, and you know me, and we are together, a community.

We collected more of us, and they collected more, and soon we were nearly everyone, except for those who were already asleep. All quietly tiptoeing up the stairs, in our night gowns, or pajamas, or still in the clothes from the games. We followed everyone and no one and found ourselves in the forest room. We tried the recreation room first, but it was too cramped, and too close to some of the parents quarters. We tried the swimming pool after, but it was cold, and echoed, and felt eerie at night, with the wide, thick glass wall feeling like an open mouth to the outside blackness. The forest room was just right. It was big enough, far enough from the ears of our mothers and fathers, and closed enough to feel safe.

For a while, we just ran through the trees, and sang, and danced, but without our parents watching. The forest room is a quiet place, and we made it wild. We tackled each other to the sand, and tried to see how many we could lift, and how far we could leap over the plastic fires. We were laughing, and it all felt so good. Then we would fall to the ground and talk.

I was avoiding Byrn, because I didn't want to speak to him. I think I was embarrassed, but also still unhappy with him. If he drew near to Seraphina, they would become strange and place distance between themselves. He would look at me and wave, and I would look away.

When I was tired, and lying on my back, catching my breath, I saw him through the trees, against a painted wall of further trees, and he was talking to Gabriella. She is in my track, and I consider us friends, and I became angry again, but I don't know why. I didn't want him talking to anyone who was supposed to be mine. I was worried they were talking about me. And then he turned and looked at me.

But Seraphina pounced on me then, and pretended to roar, to frighten me I guess, but it just made me smile. She sat beside me and asked if I was having fun, and I was, so I said yes, but then Byrn was walking over. I guess I had a look, because she asked me what was wrong, but I said nothing. Then he stopped right at my feet and we both looked up at him. He was so shy.

He asked if he could talk to me. I said yes, and Seraphina did not move, she just watched and waited, and it felt good because it meant she was on my side. He hesitated for a while, then said, "Never mind," and then said, "Actually, are you mad at me?" And then Seraphina looked at me and they were staring at me and I realized I looked like an idiot lying down, covered in sweat and sand, and so I just sat up, but I didn't say anything.

I was mad at him. But it felt so stupid because I couldn't remember why. I just was, and I knew it was childish, so I said no, which I guess wasn't a lie because I guess I wasn't anymore. It was embarrassing so I asked him why. And he just said he thought I was. Then he kind of just stood there awkwardly, until he finally asked if he could sit with us. Of course he could have. I wanted him to. But Seraphina said we were going to begin the games soon, so we had to get everyone.

We did, and we all sat together around a fire light, and Byrn was across from me, and Seraphina told us the rules. The game was called Angels or Demons, and explained that it was a spiritual game. Because we are always pulled between angels and demons, the game is meant to strengthen our spirits. We would be offered to tell the truth about a secret, or to challenge ourselves with a dare.

We became quite cautious and apprehensive, because it sounded like temptation, which is a road to sin. Elysa quoted Timothy 2:22, which is "Flee also youthful lusts: but follow righteousness, faith, charity, peace, with them that call on the Lord out of pure heart."

But Sera is the smartest in her track, and quoted 1st Thessalonians 4:4 and 4:5, "That every one of you should know how to possess his vessel in sanctification and honor; Not in the lust of concupiscence, even as the Gentiles which know not God." We are not Gentiles, she said, and we must know how to possess our vessels in sanctification and honor, so we must strengthen them as we strengthen our minds and muscles. When challenged, we are to resist the sin of whatever might tempt our hearts, so that even if our vessels are confronted, our spirits can rejoice in God's light and protection. She even asked Elysa, "Hast though faith? have it to thyself before God. Happy is he that condemneth not himself in that thing which he alloweth," which is Romans 14:22, and explained that in verse 14 nothing is unclean in itself, and that sin only happens in the heart, so we must know our hearts well.

Elysa asked for an example. So, Sera asked if two women kissing is a sin, and Elysa said it was, so Sera quoted 1st Peter 5:14, "Greet ye one another with a kiss of charity. Peace be with you all that are in Christ Jesus. Amen." And then dared Elysa to kiss her, because a kiss is not a sin, and that only the sin of it could be the lust in her heart, which Elysa did not have.

So Elysa kissed Sera, on her mouth, right in front of everyone. I felt a stir of sin, but I did not allow it to take control. Elysa pecked her at first, but Sera took her face, very tenderly, and kissed her again, for a moment longer. When she stopped, Elysa seemed paralyzed, and was only staring at her. And Sera asked her, "Elysa Stalwright, before God and everyone, tell the truth, did you sin in your heart?" And Elysa said no, of course she didn't, and Sera told her she was stronger in the Lord, and everyone applauded her.

And the game went on. Everyone played, and we learned truths about each other, and we performed spiritual challenges, and we started to laugh, because it was so strange, but we were all so beloved by God. I dare not write the truths or dares of others, as it feels wrong to write about them now. It did not feel wrong then though.

Still, I will not, for their sakes. But I should note that what began as simple enough tests grew to be more and more difficult. We were kissing, and touching, ██████████████████████████████████████ ████████████████

What should have been crimes, weren't. We were growing spiritually, and it was good, and it was fun.

But I think I did it wrong now. When I kissed Sera, it was fine. But Erik dared her to kiss a boy who wasn't me. I think he wanted her to kiss him, but she kissed Byrn, and I want to get this right. In my heart I knew it was not what it was. But maybe I sinned. ████████████████ She kissed him, and I felt strange. It was almost an anger, or a fear, but then it was a new thing. It was like waiting for a drink in line at the water fountain. I wanted it to end, and I wanted it to last.

And then it was her turn, and she dared me to kiss Byrn, ████

When she dared it, she had those eyes on. The strange kind she gets sometimes. It was almost like she was waiting for someone to scold her, but in a way that she was excited for it. And these dares had always been funny, and exciting, but I was nervous now. We were just looking at each other without moving, neither one of us would stand to cross the fire light and meet the other. Which made everyone laugh more. I got embarrassed. And then Seraphina took my hand and stood. She was smiling, but it was so small you couldn't see it unless you knew her right. And I probably swallowed, but I forget standing and crossing the circle. I know I did but I can't remember it now. I know it took forever, and my body was freezing and burning all at once. And this is why I think I maybe did the game wrong. Because Byrn didn't stand, and I was standing over him, and he was looking up at me, and I was nervous. I had felt nervous about all the truths and dares but none of them were this bad. He was too far down, because he was sitting, and so I knelt down to be closer to him, and I leaned in and I kissed him on his lips.

I expected it to be different. I expected his lips to feel different, like a boy's lips, like nothing. I expected to feel sick, because of the sin of it. I expected it to be rough and hard. I expected to feel nothing at all, like a wall, or wood.

But I think I did it wrong. I kissed him the way I kiss Seraphina I think. It felt soft and warm like hers. It felt kind.

And I think I did sin in my heart, actually, because I kissed him for so long. I didn't touch his face, and he didn't touch mine. We didn't kiss long, actually, but it was a real one. Or maybe it wasn't and that's why it was wrong. I don't know. I was a little high on him and so his top lip was a little between mine.

And I am damned because now I keep thinking of it. I keep wanting to part his lips, and have his lip in my mouth, and to do what Seraphina did.

But it didn't feel wrong then, it felt good, and Seraphina kissed my cheek and asked if I sinned in my heart, but it didn't feel like a sin. It felt like a good prayer feels, and now I feel like an idiot. I am torn apart by it all now, and I don't know why.

I said no, and I sat back down where I was sitting, and I was warm, and being apart from him felt embarrassing. He looked at me after, and then we kept playing, until we were all tired and falling asleep, so we all left, and we didn't talk after. I wish he had. I want to talk about it now and apologize for doing it wrong. I feel so stupid.

I know it is wrong to like kissing men. I keep reading but I can't find why it is, just that it █████████████████████████████ ██ ████████████████ condemn ███████████ ██ ████████████ Is sin still sin if the sin is a thing in love? God is in love. How can God be in sin? ████████████████

kindness and love,

my wanting

[6]

    I am become an unwell thing. I must pray and seek guidance.

---

[6] Another scratched out section with the remaining pieces being what could be discerned. However, the questions regarding sin, love and God were carefully boxed in, and not scratched out.

Seraphina

from her journal

I am awake, but who's to say so? I am taken by a dream, and it washes me.
I am baptized, from the inside, in thick, warm waters, brought unto me,
from the death I drank. I used to sleep. As all the angels in heaven sleep. As
mother and father. As Harley and Byrn. As Seraphina. Her flesh, at least.
But she is in the washroom now. Her skin is cold. Her bedding is in the
washroom machine. It spins so diligently. I am spinning. And the night is
everywhere. The quiet. I become the quiet. I become Seraphina in flesh, as I
have known her in dream. In vision. In vision prophetic, or true desire,
deception, suffering. I am of the suffering flesh now, returned. I can still
feel them. It was a place of meat. A place of the raw wordless eyes. Endless
devouring pleasure. Contents. Contents, my darling, Seraphina, before they
abandon you. We begin in the middle of things. Eating. Everyone eating, so
politely. We are in the grand dining room. Harley and Byrn sit across from
me. Mother and father beside me. The whole world has come to eat. And
Harley makes Byrn laugh. He whispers to Harley, and they look at me. I am
a hungry mouth only, yawning wholly. And they unbutton their shirts. They
climb onto the table, clattering dishes and glasses astray, breaking them,
crawling unto me like needy things. They pull me up. Onto the dinner table.
They pin me to it, to the flowers and burning candles they have scattered.
To the broken glass, and the forks, and the wines and the warm foods. They
have undone my dress, they have ripped it away and I am laid in only the
under things. They grip and fumble at them, these shackles, these vices. I
free myself of them and everyone is watching. I am naked. My lovers hide
me from the eyes. They dress me in their half-nude bodies. Grabbing,
sliding, rubbing. Such needy things. Harley's hands. I know his hands, his
gardener hands. They are rough, they are kind. They are for flowers. They
squeeze my breasts, they hold them so gently. I am not a flower. I say I am
not a flower. And he remembers I am not a flower. And his gardener hands
pinch, and grip, and pull. And when I whimper he silences me with his lips
so no one can hear my secret sounds. His tongue finds mine. Then he is
impatient. He is on my neck, and my chest, and my ears and my chin and
my mouth and he can't decide where to die. And I am known to Byrn as
well. He nuzzles and crawls along my stomach. He whispers to my navel,
no words, only sounds. Another language, perhaps. A secret one. He kisses
at my hips. Then further in. Then further, but never far enough. My legs. He
finds my legs and holds them like idols of gold and fire. His tongue maps
the unholiest route to my wanting. Then his weight is on my thigh and his
chest heaving against me and my hand finds his back. My other in my
Harley's hair. I am squirming. I am the needy thing. And I hear them all

clear the plates, and everyone waits for dessert. But they cannot see me beneath my princes. And Byrn's breath warms me along my terrible place. My favorite place. But he is not afraid of it. The way we were all told be. He is kissing me. Between my thighs. The place we never discuss. The place Eve killed the world. The vulva. The labia. The clitoris. The peaceful place. And he is a jealous thing. With no lips to kiss. And I am drunk from. A blushing fountain. A secret well. And Harley sucks from me. A blind hunger. As though I can feed him from my lip. From my nipples. From the freckles. From the skin of my neck. A hungry thing. And so he bites, to eat, and I exhale in triumph. My hand is a pilgrim lost in the world. I search for his erection, but it is a forbidden thing, a prisoner, trapped under a belt, a button, a zipper, and god knows what else. I groan and he presses his hips into me and rubs his hard secret against my naked side. His erection. His penis. His secret thing. And I hear everyone eating the dessert, finally given. It smells of strawberry. But I cannot see it. I only hear the clink of silverware, the slurp of lips, the squish of my friends and my family chewing sweet things all around me, moaning with such soft satisfaction. And there are tongues in me. They are vile things. And I love them more than clean air. Or strawberry desserts. How they squirm in me. How they flick in me. Snap and dance. In my mouth. My vagina. And the hot mulled wines fill the room. Bathing me. Drowning us all. I arch. Floating inside benevolence. Then I am heavy again. Crushed under real air again. Returned, again, to my sheets and my blankets. My sweat and my baptism. My quiet laughter in the night. Harder to kill than ever.

Harley

from his journal

I have been shadowing my father today because I have no classes.
We are taking a break.

Tonight we are supping with select Leaders from the Councils of
Guardianship and Purity. I am nervous. ██████████████████
███████ The men of Guardianship are men who are known to be very
stern in the ways of God. They are tasked with protecting us physically, as
well as spiritually. They are watchmen and enforcers, both inside and
outside the walls. They are the only ones who ever leave. They are all tall,
and wide, and very strong. Father has said it is a delicate task, to keep them
both fortified, yet restrained. For we are ruled by God, but they have argued
to rule us once before.

Though that is not why I am nervous, I suppose. Not really. I am
nervous they will catch that I am skeptical. I have doubt in my heart, not in
God, but in the law. Our law is the law of God, yet they are all enforced by
men.

During studies with father today I asked him about sins and the
laws. I did not want him to misinterpret my intentions, so I shrouded my
real curiosity with generalities. I asked him, for my own strength in
specificity, what made some things sinful: Jealousy, secrecy, gluttony,
adultery, and others, but also homosexuality.

He said the sin of it was in the sexual deviancy of the act itself. It
is an abomination, and disgraceful to God's design for sexual intercourse,
he said. I understand this, as God made man and woman in the way to have
children. There is no way for men to do so.

And yet we do not obey all the designs as they are written in
Leviticus. We make no sacrifices, our meat is synthetic, our clothes are
mixed thread, our beards are shaven, we accept no foreigners, not even as
slaves, as we are permitted to do, and so I am confused as to why some
designs are law, yet others are ignored.

I think we may not know God's designs as well as we say. For
God has changed His mind in the past. He flooded the world, He sacrificed
His son, He burned the world. If all things are made by Him, and the
testaments say nothing is impure in itself, then what is our design, if not
God's?

It is a question of morals then, maybe. If the design of ourselves
is in God's image, then all things that are made are made by Him. The
mouth, for eating alone? Praising Him? We sing, and we talk, and we kiss,
and drink, and we spit, and laugh and scream and bite and I wonder then
why God does not take away anything not within His design. The hands, for

what? Holding what? In prayer? Food to the mouth? To wash? To touch, or pet, or pinch, or slap, or scratch, or what? If my entire self is designed by God then He has given me the way to do all things with it.

Things are not good or bad. Only the heart is. If my design is used for things of good, or things of love, or of joy and pleasure and sweetness, how then can it be a sin?

But this is why I don't know anything, I am not a Scholar and so I am confused why some things are sins yet others are not despite being called sins all the same, when none of them feel so in my heart. When I feel jealousy, and deception, and hate, I know they are sin.

I will pray and study further, but I realize now I have been neglecting the other design for this journal. I have mainly been reflecting on things of the spirit, but I am also to be tracking my duties and organizing these accounts accordingly.

I worry I might not be right for the Council in any respect. I find my duties dull and unremarkable. We just talk, or plan, or write things down, and nothing really ever happens. It seemed so exciting at first. ▮▮▮ ▮▮▮▮▮▮▮▮▮▮▮▮▮▮▮▮▮▮▮▮▮▮▮▮▮▮▮▮▮▮▮▮▮ ▮▮▮▮▮▮▮▮ I have even lost interest in father's sermons. ▮▮▮▮ ▮▮▮▮▮▮▮▮▮▮▮▮▮▮▮▮ I feel shame for admitting so. But it is true. They are calculated, and rehearsed, and no longer interest me. I wonder if I should feel shame for this.

I am being grouchy, I think. We did actually discuss something interesting earlier. We often do, I am just so, I don't know, forgetful, I suppose. Because we have the autumn social coming up, father was quizzing me on what I understood of it. I knew it was for the Ascended class only, I knew it was followed by the baptismal shower, and that the shower was sacred and bonded newly adult couples in Christ's blood.

He asked if I knew what Christ's blood was. I did not, and he told me it was a synthetic formula which blessed couples through chemical bonding. He said God showed it to them long ago. I asked how, but he just said chemical bonding again. He said pheromones, hormones, neurotransmitters, human chemical things that God uses to bond us biologically.

I asked what happened if someone wasn't in a couple already. He said they would most likely find someone.

I asked how, and he said they would be drawn together, spiritually and chemically.

I asked what happened if someone didn't find someone, and he said nothing happened.

I asked what if someone in a couple was drawn to someone else, he said there was counseling for that, but that it was extremely unlikely.

I asked what if more than two people are drawn together, and he said it wasn't possible.

I clarified that I meant what if someone was drawn to more than one person, and he said they would have to pick one.

I asked what happened if two people were drawn together who didn't like each other. He laughed and said it wasn't possible.

I asked what happened if two friends were drawn together. He said it was great.

I asked what if they were the same sex. ███████████ ████████████████████ Two women, maybe. He said that would have to be reported. It was sinful, after all. I said of course.

He asked if I was nervous. I said a little, because I don't really know what to expect. He said it will be simple. He said I will be drawn to Seraphina, that I will dance with her, and that everything will be fine.

I hope so. But I am nervous still. Because ████████████████

Seraphina

*written in the margins of Psalms Book 4,
torn from a Bible, and later stored in her journal* [7]

I imagine him as snow. The old kind. There is no ash in him. He is soft, and
he is quiet, and he keeps all the world beneath him. He is gone in soft
breaths, and cold, and sweet, and if I hold him, he would melt. He would
soak through every part of me. He has eyes, like anyone has. Blue, but who
cares? It's his use of them. He speaks with them. Secrets. He tells you kind,
hard words, that splash around in your brain, and it's only his eyes looking.
He has lips, like anyone might. Corners and curves. He smiles, as though no
one taught him how, and he makes it up. They make words sometimes.
When he wants you to smile. He is quiet. His words are only yours. He
gives them, privately. And you laugh because he is funny. And you laugh
because only you know it. And when someone finds him, he becomes a
play. He is now Byrn, but not yours. He is the man like men are. He is
reliable sips of warm drink. Patient and generous. They flit around him like
swirling dust. The girls sacrifice themselves upon his altar. An offering of
smiles, on offering of compliments, an offering of a touch on his arm here,
a soft lean into his chest there, a laugh – or pretending to maybe, because he
was not funny for them, not in his secret way. They would offer him
anything. But he is a cruel god. A snow on the old earth. And they float
apart from us. Unfed, yet satiated. I found him. Or did he find me? Here in
the library. Wandering like ghosts between books and old smells. He leaves
me silly acts, like berries to consume. The books are too heavy, and so his
muscles ache. The books are too boring, and he has drifted asleep. The
books are too high, and only I can get them, though I am so much shorter.
He nearly makes us troublesome, because we are choked laughing. He
blankets me in his cold softness. He treats me like a riddle. A filthy script to
be dusted and read under covers. I am getting on his fingers, and he
continues reading. He asks me things. And the girls are only glances upon
me. I am a thing for questions, and they are a thing for offering. I am a
thing for answers, and they are a thing for patience. I tell him. He is a deep
flesh to scratch upon. A soft page. And my words land sticky and hot on his
ear. My classes, my performances, my thoughts, my theories. And his seem
to grow between mine, mixing, like small flowers in gentle grasses. And I
would lay Harley there, to rest, to eat, to die, to rot so peacefully, to melt
into our little kindly world. A world of quiet teeth and notes we've slid
across the table. A world of wondering. Of kisses. Of our eventual deaths.

---

[7] Another instance of convenience. Judging from the entry, she likely wrote this in
secret with Byrn nearby.

Byrn & Seraphina

from a scrap of paper, found among his things

Why did you tell Harley to kiss me?

Because it wasn't fair.

What wasn't fair?

For only one of us to kiss you.

Seraphina

from her journal

It is still in my hair, so sweetly noxious. It is soaked into my gown, and I am only memories of sins no one invented. The children are hiding in the halls, like feral things, I hear them, the patter of secret chasing, the soft press against a wall. I am all roots, crawling through skin, searching for it so desperately. Another sip. I am broken. I am shattered. I am made mosaic of raw need and smoothness. I am a danger. Waiting for my door to be knocked upon. Softly. Quietly. So we may turn our pages in secret. I am a defective saint. Writhing like dirty things in filth. I have never eaten. I have never breathed before. I need [8]

---

[8] Seraphina has ended abruptly here. The entry page has been stained with what is presumably the Blood of Christ.

Harley

from his journal

I want to write this down before it becomes like a dream that I forget. I can still see them so clearly. They came to my door late in the night. I had showered and dressed for bed, and they were still covered in the Blood of Christ. I had been awake, thinking of them. It was a quiet knock at my door, so my parents across the hall could not hear, so soft it nearly wasn't a knock at all. When I opened the door, they were standing there, still in their formal clothes, soaked and dripping in red. Seraphina in the doorway, and Byrn leaning against the doorframe. We were told to wash as soon as we were home, but there they were, shaking, and stinking of the sweet blood. She was looking up at me, her makeup had run a bit, and it was the most beautiful thing I had ever seen. Byrn's jaw kept clenching and unclenching, and he was breathing heavily. They both were. Like nervous kids, hesitating. Seraphina went first. She reached for me, but then stopped, pulling her hands back. She bit her lip, and looked at mine. I knew I didn't stand a chance. I had felt clean, and even, safe and warm in my soft pajamas. I wanted them to destroy it.

"Hi," she said. I was still holding the door, and my other hand grabbed the doorframe, because I felt a pull, like a spell attached to my hips, and I had to stop myself.

I told her, "It's late," and she leaned into Byrn's chest with the side of her head. She nodded, so desperately, and her chest was heaving. I couldn't stop staring at them. He was squirming, trying not to nuzzle her hair. He looked at me, and I swallowed, terrified. It was like a hundred little pinches inside my torso, making their way down my abdomen. I had such a deep feeling in my hips that I wanted to fill up, somehow, I don't know how. I wanted it to be like before again, but my parents were just one door away.

But then I was undone. "We should go," she said. But it was quiet, and her back was pressed to Byrn, and he was swallowing so hard. "Do you want us to go?" But it was like a whine, like it hurt her. And I didn't answer. "Do you want us to go, Harley?" But they were inching closer, hesitating like children afraid of getting burned. "Say so. Say you want it." And she was so close I could feel the breath in her words on my lips. "Please." And she was there, her mouth open, like some hungry animal I could feed. And Byrn was holding the top of the doorframe, covering us, filling the doorway, breathing so hard it was like waves filling my ears.

I closed my eyes, waiting for a reason not to. And it took too long. And slowly my lips fell to hers. Like a small spill getting bigger. Getting everywhere. Brushing against her lips. Soft and so agonizingly slow, in case a reason not to could stop me.

But then her tongue was on mine. And I fell into them. Byrn was a blanket, hovering an inch away, wanting, and I turned to him, and I was kissing him too, and it was better than a dare again. Long, deep kisses. Slow mouthfuls of soft lips. And there were lips on my neck. And I was against the doorframe somehow. And their hands were covering me like before. So many hands. And we were this strange knot of soft little moans, and whimpers, and wet kisses. And a hand was over my pants. It grabbed my erection, and it was a heat that warmed me all over, and a shock, and my body wasn't mine anymore. I was elsewhere, kissing and touching, there in the open doorway.

And my door banged against the wall. We jumped, and there was a moment where we all froze, looking at one another. It was fear, but I remember it so clearly. They were so beautiful.

There was noise across the hall, from my parents' room, and I panicked. I wanted to pull them in, but that was stupid, so I told them to go, and they did. They kissed me and ran down the hall. And I closed my door and waited there, my heart pounding in my chest, listening for my father. But there was nothing. And I regretted not pulling them in.

I miss them. Before that, there was the dance, the autumn social, and it seems so silly now to think how nervous I was. But I was.

I was nervous going to Seraphina's room in my tuxedo. She answered the door in her gown. It was a soft pink then, and it showed her shoulders. She looked so beautiful, and she smiled because I was staring. Her parents were there to see her off.

I was nervous walking together to the gymnasium, where the Council of Youth had decided to hold the social, because it was retrospective of old-world culture. It was a funny tradition, "a promenade in a gymnasium," for young adults to dance and socialize. It had been decorated with sparkly balls and curtains. The musicians played ancient songs from the middle of the 20th century, a time before things got really bad apparently. They were slow and dreamy, and I had never heard anything like it. They always sang about love, about dancing, and holding hands, and being together. It was interesting at least, and fun to dance to. The music made us move differently. We tried to dance like normal, but the music would get so bumpy at times, when it wasn't slow, and we all kept bouncing along. It felt silly but everyone seemed to be having a good time. And the sparkling lights made everything feel magical.

I was nervous when we didn't see him. I remember we were both looking for him. We didn't talk about it then, but I think we were.

Then I was nervous when I did see him. He came later than everyone else, and he was with Elysa. She looked wonderful, and so did he, and it made sense why they came together. They're both blonde and pretty.

I remember my heart sinking, because it made so much sense, but it didn't at the same time. He talks to everyone, so of course they know each other. But I figured he would be alone, or maybe I just hoped he would. We were dancing when we saw him, and I felt Sera's hand squeeze me in surprise.

He was smiling. They both were. It was a slow song, and it made me so sad to see him so handsome. Then he saw us. I think we weren't smiling, because I saw him change. I saw it in his eyes mostly. His eyes always tell what he's thinking. It was like he felt bad. But then he smiled again, and nodded at us, like we were strangers.

Seraphina said she didn't know they were friends, and I said we were all friends, which was stupid, but I didn't want to talk about it. Then she looked at me, and she didn't say anything else, but I could see she was annoyed by how her lips came in just a little. She took my hand and led me through the crowd, closer to the musicians, where it was louder.

She danced with me, and when I couldn't keep up, she danced by herself, before me, and still with me, but wilder than myself. Sometimes she can't be held, sometimes she needs room, sometimes she is so much bigger than me, brighter, in a way, and I love it.

Then Byrn was next to us, dancing with Elysa, and I was nervous again. He smiled at us, and Elysa said hello, and I said hello, and Seraphina looked at him once, then turned her back to him and kept dancing.

When the song ended, the musicians played another slow, dreamy song, the kind everyone either held each other for, or left for. Seraphina left. She declared she was getting us punch, turned, stopped to look at Byrn, said "Hey" once, then slipped past him. He watched her leave. Then he told Elysa he would get them punch, and went after Sera. Elysa was surprised, and probably disappointed to miss a slow dance with him, but I had always known how clever Seraphina was.

Elysa turned to me and said it looked like we both lost our dates, which was dumb, because really it was just that my date had stolen her date, but I just smiled and told her I would dance with her. I think I complimented her too. Her hair or her dress or something.

So we danced together during the song, very politely, and we chatted. She was talking about Seraphina, but I was only really half listening. She was saying nice things, about how passionate she is, and unique, and interesting. Although now it seems like they were only partly nice. Like maybe being unique and interesting and passionate wasn't all good.

Anyway, I kept glancing at the punch table, where Byrn and Sera were talking. It seemed strictly polite and serious at first, their conversation. But then Seraphina laughed, and it was so beautiful, and I thought I should have been jealous, but I was smiling. I wanted to know what he said, I wanted to laugh too.

Then Elysa was talking about Byrn, about how handsome he was, and mysterious, and how much she liked him. She asked if I knew him well and I said no. She said no one really does, which was why she felt special to be with him. Which was funny because he was with Seraphina then, and they were smiling together, and drinking their punch, and I was suddenly worried they would never come back. But right then, Sera looked at me, as though she could hear my thoughts, and she smiled at me. She said something to Byrn, and they came over to us.

We talked with them about punch, about how bad it was, laughing about it, and then we danced, and talked more, the four of us, drinking punch, dancing, all together, and it was fun, and the music was great, and eventually I got tired from it all.

Elysa said her feet were hurting, and I said I wanted to sit down as well, and Seraphina said she wanted to dance, and Byrn did as well, so Sera suggested Elysa and I sit together while her and Byrn danced together, and somehow her brilliance made me feel proud. I said it was perfect, and Elysa took my arm, and joined me at a table. She seemed disappointed again, but she was still as cheery as ever. Fake cheery maybe.

I saw the two of them again, together, dancing, and it made me feel a strange happiness. He was dancing differently now. Seraphina was wild, and she was showing him how to be wild too. He danced like she danced, and they looked so odd that I almost laughed. They were having so much fun, and they were starting to shine in their sweat.

And Elysa was talking to me, but I wasn't really listening, again. She was joking about their dance moves, but I didn't laugh. Not really. She was asking if I was nervous, about him dancing with her, and I realized I wasn't at all, for the first time all night, I wasn't nervous about anything. I looked at her and I just said, "Why should I be?" but she didn't know why.

So I asked if she was nervous that Sera was dancing with her date, and she got a little red, and stuttered, but then said of course not, because Sera was with me. Then she changed the topic, very quickly, asking me when we were to be married. I said a joke, and she laughed, but I don't remember what it was. Something about how we'll get married when people stop asking.

I noticed other people were watching Byrn and Sera as well. They were either fascinated by them, or laughing at them, or confused, or bothered, or some mixture of it all, and I felt proud again, and I'm not sure why. I think because I knew them. Because I understood them. They were mine, in some sense of the word. I wanted to join them, but I knew I couldn't dance with them, not like that. It would be different then. So I just watched them.

Then they watched me, and I felt so bright and shining. And they were dancing for me. Laughing and gesturing, pretending to sing the words of the song for me, professing their undying love on their knees for me.

And for Elysa too, I guess, because she laughed as well, but I really don't think that they were looking at her.

Then it was over. The song, and the lights, and the dance. The Leader of the Council of Youth stepped up to the microphone and informed us all. He was so joyful and comforting when he spoke. He said it was time.

I remember him saying it was special, and God would be with us, but not our elders, just us, how we had done well, and to not be afraid, and to remember our morals, but to open our hearts, because we were ready, we were ready to be baptized in the loving blood of Christ.

And there were rules, but I don't remember those. Only that we had to keep our clothes on, and then go home and wash immediately after.

I was nervous again. We all were. We only knew rumors then. We had a jitteriness in us, even though we all kept very still, or tried to at least. Then we all went into the locker room, and into the showers. It was the girls one, I think. It was all very clean, and dark, and there were flowers and very dim lights along the floors.

It was quiet, and we were all huddled there, waiting. A dripping started, one shower head, then more, then a dripping from the sprinklers in the ceiling too, and I was nervous. The Youth Leader's voice came in over the speakers in the locker room. It was quiet and crackly. He called us the dearly Ascended. "May you be washed in the loving blood of Christ, may your fountain be blessed, may you rejoice in the love of your youth, may you leave your father and mother, and be joined unto your love, in one flesh."

Then all at once the blood burst forth from all over, raining down on us all, hot and beautiful. It smelled like flowers. I was startled at first. But it warmed me, and I felt so light I could float. I had to check that I wasn't. But my feet were still there, drenched, with all the rest of me. And the dim lights made everything glow and sparkle. And there were no songs playing from the speakers, but there was music inside of me. It wasn't made of instruments or voices, it was made of me, inside of me, and it tingled and moved all over me. I had never heard it before, but it made me want to move.

And I saw Seraphina, but it wasn't her. She was covered in the blood, and the flower smell was so strong and sweet from her, it kept wafting off of her. I couldn't see her as she is. I saw her as she saw herself, I saw her as I see a dream, and she was beautiful and frightening, and that made me love her. The darks of her eyes had gone large, and they were staring at me, and I was staring at her, and I saw that she was moving, and I realized that I was moving too. She could hear her music, just like me, and it made her sway and nod, and stare at me. I closed my eyes for a moment, and when I opened them, she was in my arms and we were moving together, swinging and swaying, nodding and shaking, slowly, so slowly, together, like that was how we could talk now.

Then I was aware of the other bodies, and other smells. They were all moving, swaying and dancing. Bodies holding, and bodies reaching. We were all bodies on bodies, wet with blood, and love. And then a hand was on my arm, and a head on my back. I turned and found the body holding me, looking at me with wonder. I don't remember who, but she was familiar, and she smelled sweet, like bread. Then she found Seraphina, who touched her face, and the body pulled away from me, and vanished among the dancing bodies.

There were tall bodies, like drapes unfolding over Seraphina, smelling her, dancing with her. She studied them, and they held her, but she held me. Then she was gone, and another body was holding me. She was wrapped around me, and her face was in my neck. She smelled like rich grasses, and her dance was bad, bouncing when mine swayed. And I looked for Seraphina's flower smell in the bodies. Pulling myself from the grass body. Rubbing along others in the dark.

I found her smell again, between the drapes, but she was pushing away from them, and when I wrapped myself around her from behind, she opened up onto me, leaning her head back upon my shoulder. And one of the drapes followed across her to me. He was a woody smoke smell, and his face was against mine, and his hand over my back, and Seraphina's weight was pushing me, and soon we were away from the wood smoke, moving back until I felt another body against me.

I knew this one. He was tall, and he was a deep smell, like warm spice. His back was against mine, and soon our necks were turning to find each other. His nose against my wet hair. His hands spilling across my arms and shoulders and neck. And Seraphina reaching for him. I saw his face nuzzle into her hand, and his hand cover hers. I was between soft flowers and warm spices, mixing, and spinning my mind.

I felt us dancing. Together. Three bodies, in one dance, together. And it was good.

Sera, me, and Byrn. Together. And it was good.

And then I heard a sound. Beneath the rushing blood, and wet bodies, and music inside, there was a sound of breaths, of moans, of deeply pained exhales. It was me. It was us. It was everyone. The bodies were filling hands, and filling arms, and filling mouths. It should have been terrifying. 49 bodies, wrapped in wet clothes, dancing strangely.

But it was good. It was a good dance. Seraphina's leg between mine, her pelvis rubbing against me. Byrn gripping her thigh, lifting it up, holding her. My head against his chest, my neck in his fingers. His fingers stroking me. Gripping me. Her lips around my ear, and her fingers in his hair. His hips pressing, pushing, grinding against my bottom. My hand on her bottom. Stroking. Finding. His lips on mine. My lips on hers. His mouth around her fingers. His fingers in mine. His hand on her breast. My hand on his groin. Her tongue on my neck. And the blood getting everywhere.

Then the showers stopped all at once. And the sprinklers too. And we all jolted at the silence, cold and sudden. We stopped. And I felt dizzy. I felt sticky inside my brain.

They turned the lights back on, and we untied ourselves from one other, all of us. And the Youth Leader came in, and said a prayer that I can't remember, and dismissed us, and reminded us to wash as soon as we were home, even though we were still in the showers. I guess they couldn't turn the water on right away.

There was blood everywhere. Red and thick. Dripping off of everyone. And we left little drops beside our footprints as we walked out, all of us, squishing and squeaking, together, holding each other, most of us at least, holding onto someone, holding on like we had lost each other so long ago, and only now, at last, had found each other again.

And in the light, and the looks of everyone around us, I realized we were holding Byrn.

We undid ourselves from him. It was awkward, and clumsy, and it hurt. It felt wrong. But we would be reported. So we let him go. And he walked alone, ahead of us, and only looked back, once, when he turned down his hall.

Seraphina and I held hands and looked at each other for a long time outside her door. I could hear her yearning breaths. I could smell the sweet blood. I went to kiss her, but then I stopped. And let go.

I said "Goodnight, Seraphina." But what I meant was, I love you.

She said "Goodnight, Harley." But what she meant was, stay.

And I left. And I undressed. And I put my clothes in the bin and showered the blood off. And I laid in bed. And I didn't sleep. And they came to me. And I laid in bed again. And I didn't sleep again. And I don't know what any of it means.

Seraphina

from her journal

We all choke so courteously. On the same piece of meat. Wiping our tears when no one is looking. Touching up the makeup so no one notices. Smiling. Dying. While smiling. I would reach into their throats. And they would bite me. I can see it. In the halls. In the lockers. At the dinners. They know it too. They feel it. Air in their lungs. We play our secret games, and we remember them. In class. We remember each other. And we just look away. From ourselves. Soaked in blood and they act like I wasn't there. They act like they weren't either. Love snuck out from under their pillow while they dreamt of God and Jesus and Mary. But I see it. I see their bulging throats. I see how they just want to swallow each other whole. And how they love it. The choking. It is this life. And I am the newest prayer. The newest lungs. Aching. With all this air. Shaking. In tears. We are a cup, I think, and we fill and drink and fill and drink and fill and drink and it is all of our hands. I think this is what God really may have meant. But they always kill God's favorite saints, don't they? And I think he would watch, only. How he watches us dance. How he watches us laugh. How he watches us die, then, I wonder. If I can do better. Than die. Than just watch. Be watched. Perhaps to be loved, then. Perhaps to love. Perhaps to feel. Perhaps to be felt. Perhaps. When we dance. When we laugh. When then should we die? When our kiss is just teeth? When our sweat is all mixed? When our skin is just dust jumbled in the lungs of our enemies? And it is just a crush I say to her. To that girl in the mirror. That it is just a strange crush. A strange crush for strange friends. And then a man dies. And that man has a funeral. And we wear black. And we sit in the church and we cry and we pray. And that man is dead. And his wife is dead. And his children are sad. And we are here. And we are made of such small fires. But mine keeps burning the edge of my dress when I am supposed to be sad. And my prayers are only Byrn. Kissing Harley. Lifting the edge of my dress. Knowing me. Filling me. Ending me. And so we are aching. At this dead man's funeral. Pretending to be sad. And aching. To breathe each other in. We are eyes without words. Hidden in black and condolences and serious looks. I could crawl into his casket just to shut them out. I see them, and I am nails without fingers. I smell them, and I am blood without veins. I am nonsense. I am chaos in skin. And so I leave the dead man's party. I run away. I am splitting everywhere. In my chest. In my mind. My stomach and hands. I am made of dripping urges only. I am gone, up the stairs, and hallways, and I am in the atrium at the top and it is raining. And I am raining. I look out at it. At the dead world. And the dead sky. And I am dead with it. I am the burning rains on the thick glass. Dripping down in sheets of pink. I am what the rain has become. I am the acid in the rain. I am the pink in the rain, beating on the glass, pounding, screaming in the dark sky. And then he is there, and he is my name. No, he is my Byrn. My name is what comes from his lips. And I turn to him, afraid to not be alone, for I am a crime, and he sees as much. And in his face, I see that I am crying. He comes to me slowly, like he is my father, and I am some hurt thing. And I step away, for I am a crime. And he is a good man. But he decides to be a sky. My sky. Wrapping me in himself. Holding all of my tears and my fears. And my dress is burning me again. And I look at him with the ends of my fingers. I look for the seams in his face. Where he might unstitch. Where I might find his hate for me. His lip, his cheek, and his pretty eyelashes. And it isn't there. It's only love. I want to taste his love. I want it cleaved unto me. My mouth opens to tell him, but I don't speak. And he tells me he knows. He tells me he knows in his kiss. He tells me he knows my dress is on fire in the wetness of his tongue. He tells me he knows I am the pink rains in the slipping of lips. And then there are feet on the floor, but they aren't ours. And Harley is watching in the entrance. And Byrn is afraid. And Byrn is apart from me. And no one knows if this is fine. And everyone knows that we want it to be. And Harley is upon us. And he wonders what to do. His hand slides into my palm. And his fingers reach for Byrn's. And they mix together then. And we are all close. Breathing our little fires in. And he softly puts my knuckles to his lips. Rubbing them there. And he sighs. As though I were his first bite in years. As though he could live on the backs of my knuckles. And he looks at Byrn. And joins Byrn's hand with mine. He rubs our hands. And looks at us hungrily. Pulling them down so we are drawn near. And Byrn hesitates. But we are hungry things, and we are kissing again. And Harley kisses our shoulders, and he says they will wonder where we are. But I turn to him, and I kiss him. Let them wonder. Let them wonder if Byrn's lips tickle my neck in the sacred way. Let them wonder if my privates tingle when they kiss in front of me. When I hear their quiet little moans. Let them wonder. Let them wonder who pulls away first, to return us to the party. Let them wonder why we're red. Let them wonder what we do. What I do. When I am without them. When I am still in my funeral dress. Burning. Alone, and missing them. Let them all wonder.

Harley

from his journal

I don't understand anything, and I feel like such an idiot. I don't know what I did.

One day it seems like we are something, and now I don't know. I'm so confused. We both went after her and then when I found them kissing I went to them, and it was so incredible. It felt so nice. I thought we were █████

I don't know what I thought. I must have been wrong. I must have ruined it all somehow. He probably hates me for some reason. For being an old-world thing. A ██████████

I only tried to hold his hand. Not even, I just wanted to touch his hand. I shouldn't have. That was so stupid. Of course I can't. That isn't what this is. But then he just left me and didn't look at me. He acted like I wasn't there. He acted like he couldn't hear me when I talked to him.

I remember now. I am a detestable thing to him. He finds me disgusting, and I am, and he hates me. It was because of all the stories. I don't know what to do.

Seraphina

from her journal

My Harley is asleep. And the world is in disarray. He is emptied of his tears, and his heart still lies upon my pillow. Frayed. A tattered pile. And I feel vengeful. I am full and sloshing with it. I have pieced the occurrence together and I would dismember it if ever I could. The men in our class, all alone in the lockers before mid-year assessments. They became the thing all men become when their drums are the only thing they hear, echoing, howling, devouring each other's decency. Competing with their lies. Tales of sex in the wasteland. I know them all. I know them better than they do. The poison lake filled with splashing women. They call to you, and you swim out to play. They kiss and touch, but they are hideous up close. You want to swim away but your legs feel weaker and weaker. You swim with your arms to the shore. When you pull your body out, you are melting below the navel. Skin falling off. Muscles like threads. Bones dissolving. The generous hermaphrodite. A stranger offers you kindness and shelter. They smell sweet and take you to bed. They seem like a woman, but their genitals are all wrong, and they ask you to love them from their anus, in the way men lay with men. They assure you it's alright, and so you do. When you enter the hermaphrodite, teeth in their anus chew off your penis. The flattering couple in the woods. They tell you they are married. They tell you they love you, and offer you to lie with one or both of them. When you agree, and finish, you fall into a deep sleep. When you wake up, you cannot move. They make you watch as they harvest your organs. These tales are stupid. They are vulgar and fearful. They are salt and sugar to the masculine tongues. They are infestation. And Byrn Chamberley is a coward. Like all cowards, he will survive. Like all cowards, he knows men in locker rooms never touch, are never tender, are never vulnerable. He is too pretty. He is too single. And Harley is too kind. Of course Byrn pulls away. Of course he is cold and rough. It is his instinct, and it is his genius. Byrn is a cruel god. A cruel snow. A trail of spilt blood follows him everywhere. So of course it is over. It never even began. A mistake. A coward's mistake. And I will have to wipe the tears for both of us.

Harley

from his journal [9]

All I do is wonder about him. All I do is wonder why. I just want to know, but he will not speak to me. If I see him in the halls, he doesn't look at me. I worried for a moment that I was only a spirit, unable to be seen at all, by anyone. But it's just him. It's always him.

And if I say his name, it's like it's not his name. He doesn't answer to me. It's his name though. He answers to others. It's only me.

I should feel sinful and repentant. That's why he ignores me now, so I should feel bad, and I should thank him for saving me from the gnashing teeth of Hell. But I don't care about that. This feels like a hell on its own.

My head feels heavy and hard all the time. It is filled with him. I can't hear anything in class. I can't hear father speak. I can't even hear the prayers from my own mouth. They're just words. And even God can't hear me. I ask Him to undo my mistake. I ask Him for Byrn back. I ask Him for Byrn to be emptied from my mind. But I can't hear God either. And so I know it isn't God's punishment. Or maybe it is.

I didn't mean for this to happen. I only ever wanted to be his friend. I didn't mean to fall ██████

Now I am afraid as well. I am afraid what Byrn will do now that he doesn't care for me. I am afraid what will come of me. I am afraid what my father will say. I'm afraid what he'll do.

He already knows something is wrong. It was his birthday over the weekend, and everyone celebrated today. Most everyone in Eden came. Byrn and all the Chamberleys came. And I wonder now if he put up a fight, and tried to argue not to come, but they made him anyway, because my father is the High Father. When I saw him, at first, I thought he was there to see me, which was foolish. He would not look at me.

We had it in the ballroom. We were all dressed. We had cake. And everyone said nice things about father and prayed and laughed and I forget all of it. I wasn't really there. Byrn has made me a specter. I just wait for him to care again. Pitiful.

And Seraphina does not mind, she says. Seraphina hates him, she says. She loves me and she despises him for his cruelty. And I always want to defend him. I am pitiful.

At the party I was supposed to have a speech as well. His only son and I forgot everything. Maybe I never wrote anything. I can't remember now if I did. Everyone was looking at me and I had to make

---

[9] At least three pages have been torn from his journal between the previous entry and this entry.

something up and it wasn't very good at all. Everyone was looking at me, and he was looking at father, or his shoes, or his buttons. Everyone was looking at me and I was the silliest boy underground, stuttering over words without any meaning.

Seraphina told me I looked like I cared about my father so much the emotion overwhelmed me, and so everyone would forgive me. She is my savior always. ▮▮▮▮▮

I am so incredibly selfish. It is only now occurring to me how much so. By the end of the party, I was standing with Sera when Byrn walked over to us. I was so shaken then that I missed it entirely. He asked if he could speak with us. I was so moved by the sound of his voice again, his voice speaking to my ears, that I didn't hear what he said for a while.

His voice was deep and quiet and unsure. He was looking at us. He was asking if he could speak with us. "Can I speak with you? Both of you?"

And Seraphina said no. She said no before I could even hear the words. She looked him straight in his eyes and she said, "No."

And he said, "Please?" And she took my hand, and she said no, and we left him. And I was so overcome then, not wanting to cry, that I missed it entirely. I had missed it all along.

He broke her heart as well.

Seraphina

from her journal

I hate Byrn Chamberley. His soft laughter in the library. His smile of the day. As though he only just arrived. It is a smile for the other girls. The nice girls. The good girls. The right girls. The ones he hasn't kissed. Or maybe he has. Maybe he's kissed us all. Maybe all of us are nailed to his wall. Waiting. To be useful. Worthy of his lips, parting over his teeth in benevolent smile. I see him. I am unseen by him. I slam my book closed. Everyone sees me now. Even the god king Byrn Chamberley has eyes for distasteful disturbances. And I glare at him and pray my eyes grow teeth so that I may tear his from his skull for how he looks upon me at last. With shame. With regret. With sorrow. The insolence. To look at me with sadness in his eyes. The chair shrieks as I become tempest and leave. He does not chase me this time. His heartbreak is an unjust place. He becomes a siege. Laps in gym class. I run alone. He follows me. Unholy plague Byrn Chamberley desires discourse. Conversation with his victim. Maybe forgiveness for abandoning his infant loves in the wilderness. Hey, Seraphina, can we talk? They used to be the sound of opening flower petals. Now his words are acid in my ear. And it is my turn to wear the crown of a cruel god. A god who cannot hear. A god who cannot speak. A god who rips her love away like covers in the endless night. Drink from my silence Byrn Chamberley. Fill yourself with my cold and rough neglect. And yearn, again, for the song of my voice this time.

Harley

from his journal

I used to know who Harley Valton was. But as I read my first entry I feel like he is a stranger now. He feels like a character I used to play, or a dummy I wheel out for my father. Because Harley Valton is a good son. Harley Valton is a dedicated student. Harley Valton is focused, and knows what he wants, and has a bright, meaningful future. Harley loves Sera, and God, and his community. Harley doesn't know Byrn, nor care what he thinks. Harley and Sera only ever kiss in moments of regretful weakness.

Who am I then? Who is this strange man I inhabit? Is he me? Is he an illness to be cured of? Is he staying for supper and every supper after? Is he the mask, or is he me, after all, and always has been? Am I me if I only know it now? If it's only whispers?

I think I'd like it. Being me, I mean. I think I'd like to get to know this me.

And I was kissed today. It was meant as goodbye, I think. I still haven't told Sera.

He had come up to me after morning prayer. I was shaken again when he did it. I didn't know if he was meaning to talk to me at first, and I had missed him so much, it stunned me. Seraphina had already gone to her class. That's probably why he did it then.

All he said was, "I think this is yours," and handed me a book with a bookmark in it. It wasn't my book at all, it was a small paperback hymnal for children, but he was gone before I had even figured that out. The bookmark had a note written on it, "Please meet me in the costume shop during communal study. We need to talk."

It's all I thought about for the rest of the day. I just kept looking at his handwriting. Touching my finger to it. I almost didn't go, I was so nervous. I was shaking and cold and I just wanted to go to the greenhouse to check on my plants instead. But then my feet kept taking the stairs to the theater's level.

There was no play, so it was empty. I couldn't find the costume shop for a while because I had never been. But then I was there. And so was he. And I wanted to cry right then.

But I didn't, thank God. It was just so much. It was like I was scared and happy and sad all at the same time. I had been trying so hard not to miss him and now here he was with me, all alone with me. And it felt strange, but safe, like all of these costumes hanging around us would keep us safe and keep our secret and keep us together.

And then I realized we were alone, and that was the point. It wasn't because he wanted to kiss me, and I was so sad it made feel like crying again. Stupid. He was sitting at a table, and he stood up when he saw me. He looked surprised and then relieved and then happy and then guilty and then my heart was breaking again because he really wasn't there to kiss me. I could just tell. He was looking at me like we were just two old friends who grew apart and stopped talking for no reason at all.

I wanted to just leave. But then he said, "You're here," and I was there, and that was that I guess. It seems kind of stupid now, but I was. And I gave him back his book and he thanked me.

He was so formal at first. He told me he wanted to meet here so we could talk in private about what happened, and how I obviously knew it wasn't alright, and I asked, "What wasn't?"

And I remember something broke in him, because he stuttered, then said, "What we did."

And so I asked, "What did we do?"

And he lost whatever speech he had prepared and whatever façade he had put on and said, "The kissing, and stuff," and he was saying more but I interrupted him, asking him why the kissing wasn't alright.

Then he was fumbling with his words again, and quoting the Bible, or trying to, I think he was paraphrasing, but it was about decency and homosexuality and lust and the usual stuff, and it didn't make sense so I just asked him if he liked me.

He just stared at me so I asked, "What about Seraphina? Do you like Seraphina?" and he just kind of stuttered again so I asked, "What about the baptism then? Why were we all kissing in the baptism?" and he said something went wrong in the baptism and I said, "What about before? Did you like me before? At all?"

And he was just staring at me, and it made my eyes watery, and I told him I liked him. I told him Seraphina liked him, and how much she liked him and how I could tell and how it was awful how he treated us. He said he was sorry.

But I was mad at him. I asked him if he ever liked us, but I said it like I knew he never did and that it was awful that he never did. And he told me he couldn't like us.

And then we argued. I would ask why he couldn't like us, and he'd say it didn't matter and I'd say it mattered to me, and he'd say how it was wrong, and I'd ask which parts and he'd tell me which parts and I'd ask why and he'd say that I know why and I'd say I don't and we'd get so frustrated and yell and whisper and he'd say it's just wrong and we can't and it has to end and how we'll get in trouble and I'd say says who and he'd say God and I'd say God never said it to me and he'd say the Bible and I'd say where and he'd guess where and I finally said I don't care, and he just stared at me.

He just stared at me. And he didn't say anything. And I didn't realize it during but at some point I had walked into the costume shop because we were now standing very close to each other.

He asked me what I meant and I said, "If God hates me, then He hates me." I said, "But it never feels like He hates me when I think of you." I said, "It never feels like He hates me when I kiss you." I said, "It never hurts when I see you kiss Seraphina." I said, "It only hurts when you pretend you don't care." I said, "It only felt bad when you were gone."

He asked if she was mad, and I said she gets mad when she's hurt.

And he was looking at my lips then. And he said they'd kill us. And he said my name this time. And I wanted to end this stupid argument and kiss his stupid face because it was so stupid how we weren't getting anywhere and how he was looking at my lips like he wanted to kiss them.

And we were close now. And we were quiet. And I said I don't care. I whispered it. And I reached for him to kiss him, and he pulled away from me.

And I felt cold. And I felt embarrassed. And I closed my eyes because I wanted to disappear, and because I didn't want to cry.

And he didn't kiss me. He just said sorry and left. And I was alone. Paralyzed. Standing there like a statue. Trying not to cry.

But I did. I crumbled and I wept.

And I became afraid I would be found out. And so I stopped myself, trying to at least, wiping my face and holding my breath. I wished I could be a costume. I wished I could be hung up and forgotten. Never alone, like I was alone now.

But then I wasn't. Then he was there. He was there again, standing in the doorway. He was watching me, and I didn't know if he was real at first. He was gone. Then he was back.

And he was breathing hard. And he had this look on his face like he was sorry for something so good. Like he was sorry he had the world's worst secret that he couldn't tell me no matter how hard he wanted to.

And he started to say something, but it didn't come out. Then he was walking into the room. Right up to me.

And he took my face and kissed me on my mouth, and I felt the entire world spin. He kissed me so hard that it pushed me back, and he walked with me, holding me, kissing, and me kissing him, until my back was against the rack of costumes, hugging us, hiding us.

And we kissed until he stopped. His eyes were closed, and his forehead was on mine, and he had tears on his cheeks. And that's why I think it was goodbye. He didn't let go for a while. We just stayed like that.

And he said he was sorry. But it was different this time. And when he left, it was different too. Or I was different. I don't know. If that

Don't Tell the Children

was goodbye, or something else, I just don't know. I guess I don't know anything anymore.

Seraphina

from her journal

He came to us like a frightened child, barefooted in the night, quiet in all his blood. But I was only teeth and claw. My rage holding me like a sickening sweat. And I saw Harley, his awful coconspirator, observing in chilled terror as the prey discovers the trap too late. And it springs upon me. Its claws smashing my throat with a hello. A soft and hesitant hello from the sweet mouth of a boy who knew he made a mistake. It was sorry in the shape of hello. But I am gusts of war. I am legions of ripe fury. I cannot be laid down with soft hellos alone. And he knows. So he admits his cruelties. He lays them at my feet like dead children he has kept within the walls. And he remembers their names and how he did them wrong and how he misses each of their laughs. And he tells me why he strangled them while they slept. How they were sacrifices. How we were altar blood for sins. Sins of a god we'd never met. And he brings me tears from a land of repentance. An offering in exchange for my forgiveness. For I am his mother's arms. I am his lover's breast. I am his drink after labor. His shelter in the rains. And he has missed me. And I remember then. How I am neither burning skies nor cruel gods. But a thing which kisses him. Which strokes little hearts upon his cheek. I remember. I am quiet gardens and he has missed me. And I remember I have missed him too. And I remember too how he hurt my love. How he made him feel detestable. I tell him so. But he is the detestable thing, he says. Not Harley. Byrn, the thief in the night, who stole our love away. A villain. A thing he hates. And I believe him. Because he is a thing I hate too. So my eyes are on Harley, who has forgiven him already. Years ago. Because he is the flower in the thorns. Perhaps the only one left. Forgiving as easily as breaths in his sleep. And I knew it even then. How they had already met. And fought. And my heart found their little betrayal to be adorable. How they could ever keep a secret from me. And so my forgiveness slipped from my fingers. It fell and it broke, and it filled the room with it's warm scent. And it sounded like 'Close the door, Byrn.' And he obeyed. And it was dark in the small room. Blackness. Silence. A beginning again. Nervous breaths. The glow from the crack in the door. And Byrn finding his way home. His shoes treading carefully. Such a small pilgrimage. And then he was there before me. I could hear his blood. I could smell his arms. Reaching for me. I close my eyes and I am the old idols. And he is the prayer. He is the hands upon my ribs. And the warm breath upon my ear. And Harley finds the alms. They are Christmas lights. The ones we were meant to untangle and bring to High Father. They make us angels in a closet now. Dim rainbows brushing against love. Kissing away darkness. They dance in his eyes. I hold him.

Closer. So he'll never leave again. And we look at Harley and he is smiling, and we are reaching for him, and his goodness in our arms makes us whole again. And Byrn is nuzzling my neck, my cheek, my mouth. And I blanket him with my kiss. I tuck him into my heart and hold his lips with mine. Then I whisper upon his mouth one warning for him to swallow. One promise. Never again. And he repeats it. His promise. Never again. Again and again he whispers it. He whispers it between kisses. To me. To Harley. To our lips. To our eyes. Our noses. Cheeks and necks and chests. He promises on his knees to me. Kissing my thighs over my dress. And I am weak. And we meet him upon the ground. Three sets of people who used to have names. Lungs and fingers and hearts and knees and toes and stomachs and brains and bones all finding where we fit. In each other. In the world. In ourselves. Crawling and gripping and kissing on a bed of Christmas lights. Poking us. Tangling us. My wrists are tied above my head in a string of soft colors. My dress no longer hides me. I am washed by tongues and thumbs and hips. And we are late. And we are missing. No matter how found we are. We are secrets in a world. We are Christmas lights, tangled in a closet. And they are looking for us. But the door is locked. And we have the key. And they will have to search elsewhere. They say so. Trying the handle once more. Our breaths held in hope. Three sets of hearts, tangled together, afraid of being caught. And we hear them leave and we laugh. We laugh and we are whole. And then I am hidden in my dress again. And untied. And laughing again. And soon we are returned to the world. Separated again. With a lie to tell. And Christmas lights still left to untangle.

Harley

from his journal

So much has happened since my last entry. I have been so busy with father's new responsibilities for me. It is Christmas Eve, and everything has changed since Byrn kissed me in the costume shop. I didn't tell Seraphina after. I didn't know how, and it didn't seem to matter because I thought it was a goodbye anyway.

But when he came back in that room he was coming back to me.

And Seraphina still hated him. Anytime he tried to come up to us during morning prayers she would just glare at him or turn and leave. I didn't know how to be around him in the hallways either, and I think he felt the same way. It all felt wrong.

So I asked her to help me on one of father's endless tasks he'd given me. And I left a note in his gym locker to meet me there too. I was so worried she would be mad, but she wasn't. He started crying when he apologized, and she forgave him.

She didn't say it, but she asked him to come in, and I could tell things were the same again. We all felt it, being there in the dark, alone. We had been sorting through the Christmas lights in the little storage room, and it was so dark with the door closed that we couldn't see each other, so I plugged them in. It was the most beautiful thing in the world. Just colorful, twinkling lights all around us. They were the most beautiful thing in the world. They were holding each other. It all felt right again.

Then we all kissed. But it was unlike anything before. In the baptism it was the blood and everyone around us. In the hallway my parents were just behind the door. In the atrium anyone could have walked in. But in that locked room there was only us. I can't even remember most of it because it was all so overwhelming. I was nearly so dizzy that I had to stop.

There was so much touching and kissing everywhere. We were like strange creatures, tangled up in lights and each other. Putting our hands on each other's skin, under our shirts, just to feel what was there. And it became so aggressive. I remember nails in my skin, and I think mine were in someone else's too. And I was grabbing, and I was biting. Both of them.

It was like I was hurting. I was hurting between my legs, and I kept pressing myself against them but that was all.

And Seraphina's dress had come up during the fray. She was in her underwear and her stockings, and I can't even explain the power it had over me. We just kept kissing her all over, and stroking her, and then each other, and I realized I was shaking, but I don't know why.

And then someone came looking for us, thank God, because who knows what would have happened next. I certainly don't. There's no way we could have had sex. Not like that. It wouldn't have been right. No matter if we wanted to.

We were so scared almost getting caught. Then we couldn't help but laugh. It was like we just woke up from a nap underwater. There was this fuzzy, breathless newness all around. So we just picked up all the lights, and agreed to say we didn't know where to bring them and left.

I was so worried father knew, because he looked at me strangely at first. I had to tell him it was hard to get the boxes down and that I had fallen. It still feels wrong, lying to him, but I know the laws and I know he wouldn't understand.

He's trying to impress the councils. We both are, I mean. He's been having me do so much work for all of them to prove my dedication. He says I should find an officially sanctioned assistant position before I finish classes. It seems ambitious, but he's been so excited about it.

I wish I could just spend time with Byrn and Sera. We never get to just sit and talk. I wish we could.

Mid-year assessments are finished, I passed, and it's Christmas break now. I had hoped we'd have time together, but my duties have taken up my whole life. Sometimes I'll get to see Sera in the rec room, or Byrn at the pool, but never the both of them and it's always such a short time. Tonight though we had the Christmas Eve supper, and before, during the party, we all got to be together at last.

I think it was the most fun I've ever had. We just talked and laughed. It's so strange to think that we've spent our lives not all friends. Byrn kept making jokes about all the Christmas lights that were hung up, our Christmas lights, and we begged him to stop because when someone asked us what was so funny we had to come up with something dumb and it was so awkward. We all said something different the first time, and Mackenzie just kind of stared at us which made us laugh even harder.

But what I loved the most was when Byrn and Sera would talk about something in a way I knew nothing about. They would get so passionate, and it was the most interesting thing to see. I've known Seraphina Caldwell for so long and loved her since we were kids but anytime she would talk to me about something she cared about I wouldn't know what to say and so I would just listen and be excited and ask questions. But Byrn thinks so differently. He isn't like her, but he asks different questions, and he disagrees with her, and they argue but it's so funny and happy. I love it.

Then Elysa Stalwright came over in her red Christmas Eve dress and stole Byrn away from us. She likes him. A lot. And it's obvious now if it wasn't before.

She asked him to help her pick out hors d'oeuvres to try. Which was dumb. But it worked because he's polite and has time for everyone.

Then she trapped him in whatever boring conversation she had come up with. And he kept looking over at us and apologizing by making this face where he flattened his lips into a line, almost like a smile, but not quite.

And we didn't get to talk to him again because then it was time for the communal supper and we had to sit with our parents. The Caldwells sat across from us at one end of the main table because of the betrothal, but the Chamberleys sat at an entirely different table. It made me feel sick in my chest for some reason. Like he didn't belong with us.

But of course the Stalwrights sat with them, so Elysa had all night to smile and flirt with Byrn, even though he never stopped stealing glances across the room at me. It felt like a signal that he hadn't forgotten about us.

Seraphina was less subtle. She had to turn around in her chair to catch a glimpse, which of course would mean most people wouldn't dare to try it. Most people aren't Seraphina. When father said grace, and all our heads were bowed, and hands clasped, and eyes closed, Seraphina watched him the whole time. I only know because when I opened my eyes after the amen she was still turned around and looking at him. And he was looking at her.

I wonder now if he even prayed. Or if they just watched each other instead, while everyone was thanking God. I wish I was smart enough to think of that. How did they know?

When she turned around, she did this thing where she sort of bowed her head and looked up at me, smiling. Or smirking. I don't know the difference, but it was more than just a smile.

During supper everyone asked about our plans for the future. As they always do. And we would tell them how we planned to finish our courses and then marry and work for the councils. But then I made a mistake and I think it was because it all felt off. We felt so far away, and my mind was split between the people at my table and the person missing. I kept looking over at him like an idiot. And I accidentally said that I'd be happy with simply working in Sustenance if leading it wasn't in God's plan. Which father promptly swept in to dismiss. Perhaps because father's plan is God's plan. Maybe ███████████ He said I was born to lead. I don't know what I was born for.

Growing and loving feel right. But I'm only 19.

Anyway, Seraphina saved me the rest of the meal. But anytime Byrn would laugh with Elysa, Sera would turn to look at them and then look at me with irritation in her eyes. But we both know it's just because of Elysa. I remember when we were all close. But at some point something changed. And now Elysa seems to grind against Seraphina. She was laying it on pretty thick though, to be fair, and laughing a little more loudly than she needed to.

When she saw me sigh she reached her foot across to mine

beneath the table. When I felt her it felt like falling into bed after a long day. And we just looked into each other's eyes. And I tried to tell her with my thoughts that I wanted to leave and go back to talking, just the three of us. Or just them talking and me listening. But just go away regardless, the three of us.

But we couldn't. We left after and were shuffled home with our families to prepare for midnight mass. I hope we can at least stand close to each other this time. I sound like some silly child. But I want to leave now, even though there's still time and I have to go down with my parents. I just miss them and the only thing that helps is writing about them. It's like if I put them here I can keep them with me forever.

But tomorrow is Christmas. We'll get to be together then. And all will be right with the world. I've grown them ipomea albas, little pots of them that I'm going to give as gifts tomorrow. "Moonflowers." Because they bloom in the darkness.

Just like we do. ♥

Alexandra Walker

Seraphina

from her journal

Cornelius Clarke was a teacher on Christmas day.
Cornelius Clarke loved music, and art on Christmas day.
Cornelius Clarke was a brother on Christmas day.
Cornelius Clarke was a son on Christmas day.
Cornelius Clarke was unmarried on Christmas day.
Cornelius Clarke was kind, and patient on Christmas day.
Cornelius Clarke was wise if he spoke on Christmas day.
Cornelius Clarke was a friend on Christmas day.
Cornelius Clarke was forty-eight years old on Christmas day.
Cornelius Clarke had a name on Christmas day.
Cornelius Clarke was a person on Christmas day.
Cornelius Clarke was found on Christmas day. With four words. Written. Please, don't be mad. By a student, who wanted to give him a gift the night before but couldn't find him. A student who had found comfort in the kind wisdom of Cornelius Clarke. A student who found him. In his bathtub. In his blood. And it doesn't matter how many times they say he was troubled. How many times they tell us to go home and pray. How many times they tell us to praise the birth of Jesus. How many times they whisper of his sins. Of his crimes. It doesn't matter if they want to erase him. His name was Cornelius Clarke. And they killed him. He just held the knife for them.

Harley

from his journal

Father has tasked me with cleaning up the room of the man who killed himself. Not the blood, Sanitation already took care of that, but his belongings. His sister is too sensitive to do it, and his parents are dead. Seraphina says the sister is embarrassed, and doesn't want to be associated with him, because she is already married so her last name doesn't match, and she doesn't want anyone to know he was her brother. No one else came forward either. Seraphina says it's the same reason.

I knew he was a teacher. I never had him. I didn't know about the rumors. I guess they weren't rumors. They don't tell us these things. But Sera said he had committed some crime when he was young and had been reformed. He never did it again, whatever it was, but he was, and still is, some sort of outcast.

Not literally, because he was reformed, repentant, forgiven and because God loves us all. But he never married nor had children. I guess he never had friends either.

I think he liked men. I haven't said so to Sera, but I think that was his crime. And now I have to crawl into his things, and sort through them, and clean it out so it can be used by someone new. But that's not all. Father also says I am to learn about him. That this is my biggest task yet. That I am meant to find what, or who, drove him to this. That I am to learn from it and that I am to report it to him so they can give everyone peace. Something caused this, he says, and I am to learn why.

And I am terrified. I am terrified of what I will find. And I am terrified that father knows, and that this is why he has given me this task, that this is the lesson. I have begun hiding my journal, for fear that it is being read. I can only pray that God keeps my love hidden. I can only pray that God keeps my love safe. I can only pray that God keeps my love from becoming a bathroom floor with blood left on it. Please. Please. Please.

Alexandra Walker

Seraphina

from her journal

We are only ever footprints. Smells left in each other's hair. In our sheets.
Our things yet discarded, until we are discarded. And the things live on.
Remembering us for us. We are only ever the memories of kindness and
heartbreaks. Leaving scars on the world and each other. We are only crypts
for the dead. And he will be forgotten in the crypt beneath the church. Just
like we are forgotten here, underground, beneath our church we burned
down so long ago. Eden is a crypt, and we are the old ghosts refusing to die.
As Cornelius refuses to die now, threatening to walk in at any moment. We
feel like early guests, going through his things, tidying the mess we've
made among his private forgetfulness. His toothbrush and his pillowcase.
His socks and his sheet music. A composition half finished. Books, with
pages earmarked, which I'm careful to leave down, which he'll never return
to. His favorite pages. Moments of peace, of laughter, and laughing along
with him. Falling in love with smudges and wrinkles and things he'll never
say to us. Missing our new friend. Wishing he would play us only just a bit
of his piece, begging him, we know it isn't finished, but please, Cornelius,
let us hear a little. You've worked so hard. And Harley keeps hiding his
face. He turns away as though his tears won't be mine. Asked to find a
guestlist in a room of empty plates at a party he never wanted to attend, and
he hasn't even grown a tongue to tell yet. I came to him to hold him, to
wipe his eyes, to prove our blood was still inside of us. And find the horned
black man what whispered death unto the sleeping ears of our dead friend.
When I looked under the bed and could not see the devil, I looked inside
the tub. When I looked inside the tub and could not see the devil, I looked
inside the wardrobe. When I looked inside the wardrobe and could not see
the devil, I looked behind the secrets. Hanging innocently. It was not fire. It
was not pitchforks. It was not leather wings and cackling and dark organ
chords. It was a line in the wall at the back. A line in the shape of a door.
When I pushed open the door there were no devils waiting. The devils do
not know of it. I stepped into his hushed tones, and draped myself with his
closed fingers. His secret pulling me deep. Welcoming us with quiet drums
made from trees of milk and honey, watching us from the corner with eyes
like breathless possibilities. Dancing behind things I've never seen.
Treasures from heaven. And fruits from hell. And bones from earth. Books
and books and books and books. About love. And hate. And crimes and
passions and triumphs and despair. About death. About sex. About us.
About worlds without gods. And pictures. With colors and symbols and
shapes. They share cups of gold mana unto the heart. Paintings of women.
And of places. And of homes and of touching. Of secrets. Of men and of

creatures. And things you can hold. That you feel and look at. They are bodies and they are not. They are for old gods. And machines. For sounds and for songs. For moving to and for crying to. And for feelings, which have spilled over, here, in some holy world, with no devils. No gods. Just us. At last.

Harley

from his journal

We've found a secret place. It is a room hidden behind a wardrobe in Cornelius' old quarters. It looks at first like just a single room, plus a bathroom and small kitchen, but there is an entire second room filled with forbidden treasures here. We have kept it secret from father and everyone but us.

I haven't written in quite some time; afraid someone might find my journal. It's started to feel like a thing I have to keep secret, like so much of me has felt lately. But I have started hiding my journal here in the secret room.

It has become a sort of sanctuary, a small paradise for only us. It is filled with shelves of books from the old world, from floor to ceiling, and pictures of things we've never seen. There are paintings of people, clothed and nude, just sitting, or chasing or fighting each other. There are photographs of terrifying musicians covered in sweat, leaping into crowds, and photographs of wars, and photographs of just people, kissing and smiling and dancing. There are things that play music, and Byrn has had to figure out how to work them. Different shapes go with different machines, and they play songs unlike anything I could imagine. Sometimes they're quiet and so beautiful, and sometimes they're loud and full of fury.

They make me feel things in strange ways, the songs and the pictures and the stories. We have spent days now, just hiding away in here to read, and look and explore. And dance, too. Once Byrn figured out the musical objects we started dancing together. All making up the moves as we heard the sounds. Just doing whatever, and being whatever. Just being us, unrelenting. I smile so hard it hurts. I laugh until I cry these huge, sad tears, but I don't know why. I've never moved like this. I've never felt like this. I've never felt so much.

But it doesn't compare to Seraphina. It just can't. She's become obsessed, almost. Sometimes when I visit the room, she'll already be here, reading. I wonder if she even leaves. She's read so many of the books already, she reads so fast, it's like she breathes them in. She only stops to sleep, and to tell us about them. We lay on the floor, and she tells us all the wonderful things she's found and what they all mean. And we talk for hours about it all, how things used to be, how they can be, how they are, and how we are inside it all, and how we feel and how God feels, and who God is even, and what that even means.

Sometimes I feel so lucky to be loved by her, to get to hear her mind, and to tell her mine. No one talks to us like this, none of our friends or our parents, no one. Byrn and Seraphina are the only ones. We're the only ones in the world. And the world is so big. Or it used to be. It used to be a place for us, I think. It used to have such beautiful words, things we can never say outside the room, things like fuck, and femme, and cunt, and threesome. It used to have such beautiful sounds, like birds, and wind, and screaming, and planes flying, and music just coming out of everything. It used to have so many ways to love.

And God used to love them all. Or He didn't. I don't know. But I wonder why we're here then. Why He burned it all, or if the devil did. I wonder if we haven't been tricked.

And it overwhelms me sometimes until we just lie on the ground and listen to songs about everything. Sometimes it makes me cry slow, quiet tears, that just slip out from my eyes.

And sometimes it makes me look at them. Sometimes we all look at each other when we're alone, and we get nervous. Even though we've all known each other and kissed each other we never really know what to do next. It's like we want to tell each other something but we don't have the words. And so we'll all just stare at each other, chewing our lips, and it feels like being touched with ice, except it's so warm. We will kiss and hug and touch each other until it becomes so strange and frightening that we have to stop. We know what comes next, or what's supposed to. We've all had Corporeal Studies. But we've agreed we won't have sexual intercourse. It just feels like far too much.

And I can't help but smile because I know father would be proud of me. In a weird way. Not really.

I've told him nothing of the hidden room. I've told him the task is slow-going, and may be slower when classes begin again soon. But I have promised him that I will learn what I must, that I can feel how close I am.

Truthfully I don't know why Cornelius took his life. He had such a splendid sanctuary. ▮▮▮▮▮▮▮▮

He didn't have anyone though. He had it alone. And it makes me so sad to think of him. Like that. We just missed him. I hope he found peace. I hope he is happy. I hope he is smiling down on us. Watching us. Dancing with us. Witnessing us celebrate his world. Witnessing us hold it in our hands. I hope we can hold it forever.

Somehow.

Seraphina

*written in the margins of Acts Chapter 10,
torn from a Bible, and later stored in her journal* [10]

My fingers shake as though the very air here kills me so favorably. My
heart unlocking my ribs through godly revolt. The speed of lies and devils
racing my frigid blood to end my life. I want to leave without a word. I
want my toes to leave gifts of puddled flame behind for them. Exit left,
Seraphina. Go back to your books you've never read. Go back to your
words you've never seen. You are a sinking corpse at last, floating in peace
beneath all the tiny lights. Free from the blindfold, now licking the chains.
We are all prisoners. Birds without wings. Trapped here. In class. In Eden.
In daughterhood. In hell. In the earth. In the dirt. In the ever dark. Little sips
of sun and sea and dust from stars in a room my dead friend gave to us. A
place for becoming. But here in the class. Fed black slop from a funnel to
our guts. They'll tell my mother again. Her duties are neglected Mrs.
Caldwell. Her duties as a student. As a disciple of God. Her absence is a
folly. When my only folly has been slurping and shitting such vulgar
venom, thick through my teeth for so long. Independent study, mother. The
truth, after all. Just reading, and reading, and reading, after all. Their books
have all been swallowed after all. And fate has brought me more to eat after
all. And I am taller than the ceilings now. I am wider than the rooms.
Thornier than the tongues. Heavier than the dreams. Darker than the prayer
that squelches festering promises of old hands around young throats.
Rinsing our entrails clean in our hell. Hanging them like Christmas lights
year-round. I can smell it now. The pretty rot. The musk of Satan drips
beneath the suit of skin. He walks the halls. He built them. We thank him
for it. We vomit at his feet for him, and we thank him for it. For the chains.
For the blindfolds. For the traditions. For the quiet. For the dead piled on
the roof. How happy mother is to hold my neck under the water. Smiling so
thankfully. How happy father is to saw my limbs from me. Singing so
peacefully. In our world made of death and deception. Take me home to my
books again, Cornelius. Take me home to your little island in the flames.
Tell me I am the only god inside. Tell me the branding scar is cruel gossip
and that only flowers can sprout from my wounds. Tell me I'm not a dirty
menace after all. Or do. Tell me anything. Tell me who you were. Tell me
it's okay to read your journal. Tell me it's okay to know your life. How you
colored your pain and made music from the filth. How you went wrong.
Tell me, Cornelius. Please. Tell me how to live in hell.

---

[10] Here, Acts 10 may have been selected purposefully to write upon as it features a
man named Cornelius.

Harley

from his journal

We found his journal in a drawer. Seraphina and I would not open it, so Byrn did it for us. I think he might not have a journal. He said it's what Cornelius would want, for his friends to remember him, and know him. I guess we are his friends now, in a way.

We cried a lot. He was so kind, and saw so much beauty in everything. He was a little funny too. But he was different, the way we're different. And I started to get scared, because there was someone he loved, and they stopped loving him. Or maybe they never did, I can't really tell. But it seemed like they did. Anyway, it reminded me of Byrn pretending he didn't know us, and it made me scared that it could happen again.

But maybe not. I hope not. The way tears filled Byrn's eyes when he read that stuff, the way his voice caught in his throat, I think he knew, and I think he felt awful. We didn't say anything. Seraphina held his hand though. He just cried harder, and we had to stop.

It was when Cornelius was younger. He had a friend in his art class named Theo, whom he loved very much. There are pages and pages of poetry about him, and about how he makes Cornelius feel. It's so beautiful. They would spend time together, laughing and writing and wrestling and even falling asleep beside each other. Cornelius would wish to be married to him. He was his best friend, and he loved him, but they couldn't be in love. Just like we can't.

Before it all blew up, Cornelius and Theo kissed. They said it was practice for their future wives, and it meant nothing, and it wasn't sex. But then they kept practicing. And then it was more than kissing. It was touching, and mouths on each other, and orgasming, and then holding, and falling asleep in each other's arms. It was beautiful. And it still wasn't sex. But Theo still went to the council after.

He said Cornelius provoked him to sin. Even though it was Theo's idea to practice. Cornelius was punished. So was Theo, of course, and he had to switch tracks, but they had to convert Cornelius. And conversion hurts, he wrote. But then he wrote, "Not as much as seeing him."

I keep crying about that. I keep thinking what I would say to Theo now, to Theo Woods, if I ever saw him. None of us know him. Either he's dead or he just isn't social like our families. We say we want to find him. But what would we say? What could we say? Fuck you, Theo Woods? You outlived Cornelius, you survived, congratulations, you lying filth?

I don't think I want to say anything to him. I just want to be everything he wasn't. I want to say everything he didn't. I want to love, in defiance of his crimes.

If anyone ever reads this I want them to know we loved each other.

But also I hope no one ever reads this because, wow, how embarrassing, please stop reading this, this is where I keep my secrets.

My favorite secret right now is when we weren't reading the journal. How we were comparing ourselves to the people in the paintings. Undressing ourselves. Shoes and socks, then shirts, then pants. Her dress and her stockings. Looking at pictures of people who died or maybe never really existed. Looking at their arms and their stomachs, and how their skin pulled at their muscles when they twisted. How our skin did the same. How Byrn's muscles peak and plunge. How my bones curve and my veins trickle down my arms into my hands. How Sera's hips turn, and her waist tucks. How our goosebumps and little shivers make us real.

Standing in our underwear, so ashamed and embarrassed until suddenly we weren't. They told me my collar was beautiful. We told him his navel was cute. We told her we loved her toes. And then our breaths got heavy, tugging at the last bits of clothes still keeping secrets. Places we suddenly wanted to share, but were too afraid to. Looking at the naked people in their soft little colors and lines, and making little jokes about how we weren't like them, until finally we would say, "Well, what is it like then?" and then we were naked people too.

And I remember being stuck for a moment, and my head feeling light, and the feeling of some kind of blanket inside of me, almost like it was brushing me down with warm strokes along my skull and my spine and my ribs. And it prickled my stomach, then buzzed between my thighs.

They were the 2 most perfect people. They made sense naked, uninterrupted by weird shapes and patterns, just skin and curves and hair and nipples. The way our stomachs slid down to our privates, welcoming our eyes. We were all so different from the people in our pictures, and yet alike at the same time.

I was embarrassed at first, because of my erection, but Byrn's penis was too, so it was okay, and so we laughed a little, but not because it was funny. It was something I don't know how to describe. It was just sweet. It was like something delicate at first. All of our eyes on each other, shifting our weight from foot to foot, and our breaths getting thick.

And Sera asked us to stand beside each other, so we did, shoulder to shoulder, holding hands, Byrn and I. She looked between us, and told us to stand like David in the photograph. We did, or tried to, and it made us laugh again. Only a little though. We couldn't get it quite right, so she came up and moved us with her hands.

Then she didn't let go. She just slid her hands down our stomachs, and our groins, and her wrist brushed against us there. It was so soft and yet it made my muscles tighten. Then she whispered to us, "Can

I?" And we said yes. And she stroked her fingers along us there, and I couldn't breathe.

She held us, and rubbed, and watched our faces with her mouth hung open, like she was amazed and so curious to see us so helpless. And Byrn moaned and pulled himself to her, holding her, and he grabbed my hand with his and pulled me to them as well.

And I was outside of my body then. I was in theirs. I was only so far as the softness of our warm skin pressing against each other. Our hands on each other. It was only softness everywhere. And little moans and heavy breaths between our desperate kisses. I remember my face in her hair, and my hand on his erection. His sex. His cock. His dick. His whatever they called it then. And it had become slippery at the end which confused me, but Seraphina told us she had read that it was normal.

Then she proved it. She put our fingers on her sex. Her vulva. Her pussy. Her cunt. Her whatever they called it then. And it was wet there too. And it was so warm. And we were petting her, and she was moaning, and it was all so warm. My head became warm too, and light, as though it would lift right off my neck.

And it scared me. I thought I was dying. I couldn't breathe or think or see. And I didn't know what to do next. I didn't know what was okay. I still don't. I've never even touched myself there. We aren't even supposed to. Not like that. Only to clean and use the bathroom.

I don't know about orgasming, or climaxing, or cumming, or what the difference is between them.

I pulled away from them and sat down and they asked if I was okay, and I said I was, but then I noticed it was time for dinner. We'd been there for so long, so much longer than we meant to be. Time had just disappeared. And I said so and we agreed we should go.

But Seraphina seemed frustrated. Not angry, but sort of irritated, aggravated. Not at us, but just something. And Byrn seemed sort of lost, sort of like me, like he'd been turned around too many times and had forgotten where we were.

So we got dressed and we kissed once more before we left each other. And I went to dinner, and I couldn't get the feeling to go away. I couldn't think about anything, or listen to the conversation with our guests, or even remember why we were meeting. I just wanted to see my loves again, and touch them, and be touched.

But then father asked me about the room, and progress, and I had to snap back into myself to remember what I was supposed to tell him. Something about beginning to understand he may have been sensitive and ashamed, but not being sure about why. And it hurt my heart to talk about Cornelius like that, which finally calmed me down about what happened earlier.

I don't know what to do now. I wish I did. I suppose I should pray. I guess I will try.

Seraphina

from her journal

It's so quiet in our secret church. The bells have all gone. And the angels
are asleep. My darling boys. Clinging to me still. Just in case tomorrow
isn't real. Their sinful arms around my sinful skin. Like vows to us. Like
gifts lain upon my softness. A head for my thigh. A head for my stomach.
And wet little breaths to blanket me in their lovely warmth and sleepy
dreams. To float into our heaven of moans and memories. Our cathedral.
Made from spit and sweat and wetness from within. Forsaken garments for
floorboards. Wrinkled bed sheets for walls. A sacred little schoolhouse for
such eager little lambs. When all the books were burned and all the teachers
shot, so many lies ago, who then could shepherd us? Who could feed us in
the night? Pawing in the mud. Shards from ancient swords. Splinters from
dead men's spears. We forged ourselves into gods with them. Found
ourselves here, in the quiet light of distant suns. And who would hold their
hands? Who then but me? Guiding them. Arming them. For they give us
fruit without seed. And no sweetness for the tongue. No wonder god
forbade it. How dumb they keep us here. Shivering and malnourished. How
frightful we have become then. The terror of our love. The horrible sounds.
The menacing smells. The awful scent of sweet fruits that fill our bellies
with seeds. And threaten to grow us into trees ourselves. A specter of sex
haunted us. It pinched our ribs and pulled our toes and howled at us until
we howled louder. A fear of everything we do not know. No more. It's
never scary once you've found it in your hands. In your mouth. In your
nose. In your veins and lungs. And oh their holy lungs. Lungs I would wrap
with ribbon and promise. My darling boys. My hungry men. My Mr.
Valton. My Mr. Chamberley. So scared at first. On your knees, I say, before
me here, and on their knees before me here they sit. Their waiting eyes. For
teacher to give them their sweet. At last our demonstration begins.
Corporeal Studies II. Reach up my dress. Pull down my stockings. Remove
those underthings. They called them panties once. I have no use for them.
Not now. Not as a I sit before them. Not as I spread my legs. As though I
were their queen upon a throne of hope. And in one hand I hold a book with
secrets. And in the other show them where to touch. The clitoris. The labia.
The vagina here. A volunteer, I say. And they are such eager little lambs.
Such frightened little fingertips. I put them where they want to go. I tuck
them in. Music plays inside my nerves. When I look, I look at them, and
they look upon the face of god. And I am an encouraging god. A helpful
god. A useful god. Yes. Faster. Like this. Now this. Now closer. Further.
Until the words aren't necessary. And we speak the sounds of angels. The
breathy whimper. The throaty groan. Soundless jaw. Tight and open. The
crinkled brow. The disappearing eyes. Gone away like all the rest of us.

And their determined little grunts. The slippery rhythm of their charity. Until the floor cracks apart and swallows me. And everything I used to be. Eaten alive. Sinking through such hot honied milk. And they are so delicate. So tender then. My sweet, they say, are you alright? Are you okay? And I am made of such fine laughter then. Stitched so delicately with warm lights. And I hold them close to me. These promised men. I am born anew, I say. I am magic, I say. I am the endless space, I say. And class goes on. For I am a giving god. A god of tongue and fingers, and oh, all the fingers we have. How useful fingers are. To scratch and pull and wrap and tug. To pet. To fill. To fill and fill until you miss them when they're gone. Put them in my mouth. Put them in my cunt. Put them in my ass. And tongues. Such soft and kindly fingers after all. Such useful little things. To taste and lick and love, after all. And hands. To spread. So many things to spread. To open and to find. Such deep desire waiting to be found. To be touched. Treasured and crucified. To crucify me with, darling. My collar, my throat. Like sacred stones. These consecrated shrines of mine. This edge of my ear, this navel, this nipple. Now his. Now yours. Now here, his back. His ass. His tired thighs. And soft along his waist like pilgrimage. His stomach and his hips. Such hallowed ground. And gentle now. Upon the altar here. Devotional. Warm and firm. Everything we've learned. Such stupid boys. With cocks they never learned to use. Hold him here. My puppet, please. Let me pull your strings. And do as I do unto you. Beckon him here. Welcome him there. Offer him this. Twist it like that. Now you with yours. And him with his. Watching you watching. As god imagined you would do. As I whisper in your ear. Such horrible secrets from heaven. And feel your lungs retreat now. Feel your muscles run. Feel your brain pop and melt and flood your corpse with the tingly everything you can't escape. Untie those painful sounds. Those strange sensations. And laugh with me. How miraculous. How far it goes. How dramatic. Your excited cum. How well you've done. How lovely. And kiss me now. And hold me. Mix your sweat with mine. And drift asleep upon my breast. Here. My darling angels here. So quiet in our secret church.

Harley

from his journal

I am in love. I don't know how else to explain this other than to say that I am in love. They are my closest friends. They are my only friends, I'm starting to think. They're the only friends I want.

███
███████████████████████████████

I feel shy, writing about them. It feels now like it felt then, like some kind of delicate thing to be gentle with. It feels like something we imagined.

We made love. That's the only way I know how to say it, and I don't even know if it's right. It wasn't sex, or intercourse, at least not in God's idea of it. It was just bliss. We were in bliss. Our bodies are made for these things it seems.

I love them. Byrn Lewis Chamberley. Seraphina Caitlyn Caldwell. Harley Justice Valton.

It was nice. We were in our secret room and we were giving each other these gifts of ourselves. Our touch and our warmth. Our bodies. Our love made into soft acts of beautiful pleasure. Perhaps we have sinned in someone's eyes, but it mustn't be God's. It must be a mistake. If our love is a sin then Hell must be a beautiful place.

I make myself laugh.

Our love. I can't even make it make sense in words. Seraphina would know how. She knows about poetry. Byrn does too, but in a different way. But I don't even know how to say what we did. I'm afraid to, I guess. To put all of those glowing feelings into square little pages.

What even would I say? Corporeal Studies II. How funny we are. Seraphina's funny little students.

It seems so odd now, how lovely it was. How simple. How we touched each other. Touched ourselves. How we looked. How we kissed and we used our tongues. And we knew these things about each other, and about ourselves, or at least I did. It felt like it did in the showers, the blood, but different. It felt like more. It felt real. It felt new.

Such new feelings. Such a wonderful place. The soft and warm embrace of someone who knows you like they know a secret. The secrets we learned. The newness.

And I feel new. Like something else entirely. I feel unburdened by something I didn't know I carried.

But I miss them now, Byrn and Seraphina, Seraphina and Byrn. My Mr. Chamberley and Ms. Caldwell. It's silly, really, how much I miss them. Not just when I'm alone. When I'm in class as well. When my fingers are in soil. When food is sweet. When tea is too hot. When I trip and they don't see. When there's a joke. When there's a gripe. When I roll my eyes. When I breathe. I miss them always.

What a fool I am, after all. For falling in love. How wonderful it is. No wonder they've forbidden it. ♥

Seraphina

from her journal

Here in my room there is a window which does not open. There is a light behind the frosted glass which glows and fades. There are curtains that hang beside it. There are flowers and rabbits in the wallpaper. There is a bed with posts. There are little birds on the blanket. There are pillows. There are my dresses in the closet. There are my books on the shelves. There are my jewels in the drawer. There is me in the mirror at my desk. There are no flames. There is no smoke. And all of it is wrong. I look at her and wonder why I must pretend she is me. I do not know this girl with black hair. And spots on her face. And eyes that never speak to me. She looks for the ocean. She looks for the breeze from far away. She looks for the smell of cornfields in summer. She looks for the flames and the smoke and the shrieks and the cackle of demons. And everything is wrong. We are in Hell. We've dug so deep to hide from God's wrath. We dug ourselves a pit. Why are they so happy? Why is there no fire on my skin? Why must I be whipped with smiles and prayers and lies meant to comfort us? It is all wrong. My island of peace. I swim through lakes of bile and broken glass for single heartbeats of old light. I stand on my toes and sip small liberties, such ecstasies, until the night wraps chains around our teeth again, and pulls us back again into the hell our parents built for us. Sit me in the lap of my lovers, not the schools of prisoners. Give me fires please. Give me smoke in my mouth if not my lover's tongue. Give me spikes to throw my heart upon before another future here. My mother's voice. My father's smile. So proud of Seraphina, faithful saint and daughter of some god who bore her in a grave. How they rattle like tired machines. How they tug at her sleeves and smooth down her hair. An internship. O hark, how the Lord hath blessed us with such bounty. An internship in the council of Purity and Law. Her future is secured. Look how tightly the lock fits upon her throat. She is such a pretty prisoner tomorrow and tomorrow and tomorrow after that. At last. And all I asked for was fire and smoke. How incredibly fucking disappointing.

Harley

from his journal

I am frightened. Everything has become so difficult. I can feel the end drawing near. I can see it. There will be a trial before Purity, for coveting another man's wife. I don't even really know them. Sebastian Smith and Annabeth Williamson. The verdict is practically decided already. They were caught together. The sentence is the question now, and I feel this feeling all the time now, like crying or being sick to my stomach. Exile? Dismemberment? For both of them, or only for her? Will that be us one day?

I understand Byrn's fear now. It seems like so long ago. Of course we can never be together. It will end forever when he is married. It is inevitable. He already leaves us to see Elysa. He has to. He can't be a bachelor forever, and he can't be married to us. He doesn't even like her really. Not like that. He likes everyone, and everyone likes him, but he doesn't love her. She's nice, he says, but she's so damn dull. His words. He apologizes to us every time he's away with her. He says he has to be with her. And he does.

And we miss him when he's gone. He's become a part of us. When it's Seraphina and myself it's peaceful, and lovely, and joyful. But when it's Byrn and Seraphina and myself it is complete. I don't know how else to explain it. When Seraphina and I make love in our holy way it is good and it is sweet and I love it and her, and yet we miss him in this strange way. We even say so after, how we miss him, almost like we're guilty for sharing in this special thing without him. How he would love it. Because it makes sense when it's the three of us.

And yet we have to pretend he doesn't matter to us. We have to ration our smiles in the hallway. And forbid holding hands. And be careful how familiar our conversations are. I see their eyes on us when we're not careful and I fear them. My blood drains from my face and my chest and I get cold with fear. I see them wonder, and then hide their suspicion behind clean smiles. And I hate it. I hate being a secret. And yet it's the only way. He is our secret room behind a closet. I understand Cornelius so well now.

And that is my secret as well. And that secret is closing in around me. Father is pushing me to finish with the room. We've nearly finished cataloguing his room, with no answer to his suicide, and will have to start boxing up his belongings to make the room available. I don't know what to do about the secret room. I can't think about it. Everything is closing in around me.

And Seraphina cries sometimes. She doesn't make a sound, but tears fall from her eyes, and she won't tell us why, but I think I know why.

Don't Tell the Children

Everything is closing in around us all.

When Byrn marries, life will go on, just the two of us, and it will be good, and full of love and happiness, and yet he will be missing. He will be a memory. He will be a shadow we must pass every day without regard. Or he will be on trial before Purity with us. He will be our Theo Woods. Our Judas Iscariot. He will have to. Our love or our lives, in the end one will die.

Seraphina

from her journal

I cannot compare him to the seasons, yet he is like the old sky, and we are doomed to wear his warmth fewer and fewer as he fulfills his godly obligations in faraway kingdoms with faraway queens. We have no seasons still. Just endless light and comfort to remind us how misplaced we've been. How I yearn for old skies. For old worlds. For old softness to hide and coil unto each other within. How gluttonous am I? So hungry I must be to love two men so endlessly and miss two men so desperately when they are not beside me. When their knuckles are not pressed to mine. When their scent is gone from my mind. When must I find the end then? Surely it is there. Surely we can find the edges of our love before they kill us. Rip us from his arms and sew him to his holy match and pump her blood into his own so as to flush us from his memory. The poison we must be. When I only want to know how we can break each other's hearts without the world doing it for us. When I only want to know what our arguments must taste like after we've forgiven one another. What our goodnights must sound like when goodbye isn't hiding just behind the curtain. What funny shape our family makes when, finally, we notice no one has left yet. I want to know what us we can invent when I don't have to miss us every day. I only want to know.

Harley

from his journal

The trial was today but we did not attend. We played house instead. It was Sera's idea. Because father had to oversee the proceedings their suite was empty to us, and so we cooked ourselves a dinner in their kitchen. Just the three of us, in a normal kitchen, doing normal things.

It felt strange at first, because we were not hidden in our secret room, I kept listening for the lock. But they reminded me the trial had set hours, and father could not return before. And even if he did, what harm had we done? Cooking. That's all. And talking.

It was so nice. We cut vegetables, and filled each other in about the trivial details from our day. We nearly burned the vegetables, and it made us laugh. We overcooked the pasta, and it made us laugh. The meat came out chewy and salty, and it made us laugh. We had no idea what we were doing, and I loved every bite because we'd made it. It was awful, but we didn't care. We talked about that too. And we danced to no music. And Sera tried to remember the words of her favorite song from the room, and we tried to hum the sounds of the music.

And we wondered about the other families. If we could be a family. If Elysa could be our family. If there were families outside who loved each other, or if they just ate each other alive. We don't even know if there's really anyone good up there, or sane, or human even. I hope God wouldn't keep them cold if they were.

And we joked with each other too. We pretended to be characters from our books. We did funny voices and Sera nearly peed herself laughing so hard. Byrn can be so funny, I don't know where he comes up with it. We told stories too, about things that happened to us. We made up stories that we wished would happen to us. And we made up our whole lives then.

We were mothers, Seraphina and I, because we agreed Byrn was definitely the father, and I made more sense if I were a mother too. I didn't mind. Mothers are so important.

And I was so afraid we would make love. They even went into my parents' room because they were curious to see what it looked like, and I was so terrified. Seraphina even looked at me and wiggled her eyebrows up and down at one point, and I must have made a face because she laughed at me then. But finally they left and we closed the door.

We poured some of the scotch my father has, just enough so he wouldn't notice, and I got so worried again but Byrn put water in it so it looked the same. We hated it. It was so gross and we joked it was because we weren't holy enough. This was how they'd catch us. We drank cola instead. And then he told us about Theo.

He was on a utility floor with his class, someplace far below, and he said he heard the name Woods. Someone called and this man answered. Byrn said he kept watching him, and he said he looked so familiar. He said he looked like he'd imagined him from Cornelius' poems. For a while Byrn didn't say anything but then when his class was leaving he walked up to the man and he just said his name, he just said, Theo Woods. And the man looked at him and said yeah. And Byrn told us he couldn't think of anything to say. He said he looked so small in real life, so disappointing and plain and unimportant.

He said he didn't want to end up like that, but he didn't know how. None of us did. So we just picked up our plates and things and washed them in the sink and dried them until the squeaking of the plates made us smile again.

Then we just sat together on the kitchen counters, talking about nothing until we knew the trial was over and we had to leave. We kissed and hugged and said goodbye and didn't make any promises we couldn't keep, no matter how badly I wanted to.

But I'll put them here. I promise we will escape and live together in a house we build on the earth. I promise we'll be happy and do whatever we want, and wear hazmat suits all the time, I don't care if we can't breathe the air. I promise we'll do this every day until we're so old it doesn't matter if we die. I promise. I promise. I promise. I promise. I promise.

Seraphina

from her journal

In our world we tiptoe around all the kingdoms still in bed. The sun comes up after the party ends. We know each other's clouds and shake the fluffy wild from our hair. We sneak into that house so far from the suburb and the city and the country. That house we built on a comet. That comet we asked to be a forest. That forest we filled with flowers like lullabies and little rivers we could walk in. And a window in the kitchen with its soft pink curtains. And a world floating by outside. We decided we could all be mothers and we could all be fathers and we could all take turns if we wanted to. We were husbands and wives. We were grown-ups and lovers. We kissed to songs we remembered and danced to memories we'd never had. I would die for them. I would lift up the sky every night and I would hunt for animals in a grocery store and I would build them a nursery for the babies we'll never get to have here. I'll wrap Christmas presents every morning and promise not to burn the food again and even learn to drink the lightning like the real women do. I'll be as happy as god intended if he could just leave us be for ten fucking minutes. I would paint the walls yellow and pink when we were pregnant, but only if Harley had the baby. I would pay the bills and play the pranks on Byrn that make him laugh that noisy laugh he has. I'd even take a mistress, and introduce her to them at a picnic by the beach. We'll keep the checkered tile, we'll play love songs in the morning, and we'll fuck in our bed on every Sunday while the neighbors go to church. We'll vacation with Cornelius. We'll throw pool parties for our daughter. We'll barbecue when the firm gives me that promotion I've worked so hard for all damn year. I'll give birth at last to twin leviathans and introduce our parents when we dig them up so they can see how proud we are. And when the party ends this time, we never have to leave.

Harley

from his journal

It's Byrn's birthday. We got him a tie, which was only possible because Seraphina's mother works in Garments, so she could get him a special one in blue. We thought it would go with his eyes. We also drew portraits of him, but we're terrible artists so they came out horrible, which made them very funny gifts. I don't know why we did that, it seems stupid now. I think we wanted him to laugh. We didn't see him open them so I don't know if he did or not. It doesn't matter.

They had it in the smaller ballroom, even though he didn't want that. When we arrived, he whispered to us that he wanted to have it at the batting cages in the entertainment wing. "But Claudia's swing is just awful, so she'd never allow that." We laughed. Claudia's his mother's first name, and he loves to call her that when he's joking. It's bizarre how he's their son. Maybe that's mean to say, but they're so serious and he's just not. I mean he is, when he's around them, but he's not really like them. That's why it was in the ballroom, you dummy, you're 20 years old now and your parents are so serious.

Even his brother is serious. We'd never really talked to him before. But Byrn introduced us to him. He's older, and a doctor, and likes playing tennis, and that's all we learned from him during our conversation.

Then Seraphina left me alone. She had to be registered for her key card as part of her internship. I still don't even have an internship. She didn't seem excited, which was odd. But I guess not. She seems to be interested in more than just councils and assignments and graduation.

Either way, it was me and everyone else in the world with a crush on Byrn Chamberley. I don't even know why I'm writing this. I don't know why I write any of this.

His parents practically announced he and Elysa were betrothed. Not officially. They didn't say it. But they always made sure she was with him. And they kept talking about her, and how well they get along, and how they love her and the Stalwrights and can't wait to be family.

So I was alone, and he was with his girlfriend, his real girlfriend, and everyone was so happy for them, and they kept saying engagement, and he wasn't looking at me, and then we were singing happy fucking birthday Byrn Chamberley and he wouldn't look at me and I felt like such a fucking fool. I'm not proud of it. I didn't run, but I did sort of rush past people. I hid in the bathroom because if I didn't I would have cried like an idiot in front of everyone during Happy Birthday, which would have looked so stupid.

And I was hiding in the bathroom and I was trying not to cry and it wasn't really working but at least I was alone. And I saw myself and I hated myself for being so pathetic.

Then the door opened because I forgot to lock the door and so now someone was coming in and I turned the faucet on to wash my hands to pretend everything was fine and I apologized and said I was almost done but it wasn't someone. It was him. And he let the door shut behind him. And he just looked at me with this sad look. And he didn't say anything, and I didn't say anything. And he locked the door. And we were alone. And I looked away. I watched the water run down the drain. Just run away and disappear. I think I wanted to do that too. I turned it off, because I couldn't run away.

He told me to look at him. But I didn't. So he came over to me and stood behind me so he was in the mirror. But I was trying so hard not to cry because I think I cry too much for a guy. He put his arms around me and his head on my shoulder. I was trying to explain why I left but I couldn't get the words out and he said he loved me. And I realized he'd never said it before. I knew it, but he'd never said it, and it was this strange feeling. Like when Adam named everything. Byrn named this one. So I looked at him, because I couldn't not look at him. And I couldn't remember if we'd said we loved him to him, or if we'd just said it to each other, or if I'd just though it to myself.

He asked if I loved him. I said yes. He said to say it. I said it. I said I love you. And he turned me around and he said, "Then that's all. That's all." And I kissed him quickly before he could take it back. And he pushed himself against me and held my face like he likes to do. I had to hold him and brace myself against the sink he kissed me so hard. It's like he puts his apologies into his lips instead of his voice.

And I had missed him so much I wanted to feel him but his stupid shirt was tucked in so I had to yank it out of his stupid pants just to get my hand up it and feel his skin. His back is so warm and big ████████████

And because I'd put my hand up his shirt he thought it was only fair to put his down my pants. He's always like that. If you hug him he'll kiss your cheek. If you lick his lip he'll bite yours. His trades are never fair. I'll never complain.

And so it rolled quickly into something passionate, the way it always does with him. His hand around my cock and his mouth on my neck and I couldn't get his stupid pants undone. And we'd just been singing Happy Birthday with his family. And I'd just been trying not to cry. And he'd said it first and I couldn't remember ever saying it so I said it in between our heavy breaths, I said it in a whisper, I said I loved him, and it was out loud and he said he wouldn't leave us. He said he wouldn't ever leave us again. Because he promised us. He promised, never again.

And the door handle turned. And it jiggled. And someone

knocked because it was locked. And we froze and it all went cold, like it has so many times before. And we stopped and he said he'd be out and he just had to help me because I felt sick. And we put our clothes back in order, and our hair, and we flushed the toilet to pretend I'd used it and ran the faucet to pretend again.

And I didn't look at him. And he asked if I was okay and I just nodded because I didn't want to lie with the same mouth that just said I love you.

Because I know it will always be this. It will always be locked doors. It will always be hiding and secrets and lies and pretending. The only world for us is made of ash and fire and death. We'll only ever be happy in Hell.

Seraphina

from her journal

I am not the lyric of a love song. In the darkness. I am not the smell of melted butter. In the scrape of the lighter. I am not the tickle of my lover's eyelashes. In the flicker of the candlelight. I am the devils. In the mirror. The favorite ones. In the dark reflection of their eyes, of hers, of that girl I used to love. The one I thought could love me back. The one who used to offer me her secrets. The one who put my crush beneath a pillow, like a wish, and smothered it until she lay still. I didn't mean to frighten her today, but how easily we're meant to frighten here, and how Elysa loves to be frightened in the end. How pleased she was to talk about the trial. How thrilled they were for justice to be done. For god's holy punishment to be brought upon these perfect lambs caught in perfect adultery. The brilliance of it. To unmake a human. To absolve ourselves of evil when we murder such a thing. She used to be a woman. That woman. A name. An Annabeth. But now she is a sinner only. Unmade in personhood, and soon unmade in life. The vile genius of it all. And for what? Sex with the man who made her an object of his lust. A woman. An object. A sinner. Her poor husband. His poor wife. All because she were made of knees and hair and fingernails. The poor fool. Agreeing to desire with some man who might be caught and blame his lust upon her voice. An affair for two to be paid by one, and one alone, with death. That once woman, once Annabeth, now sinner, to be hanged and dear Elysa calls it justice. Licks it like a brick of sugary lie. Mewling on about her god's eternal love and wisdom and justice justice justice justice and how she looked as though I'd struck her in the mouth when I said that she was wrong. It was a trap I laid and fell upon myself. I should not have done it. But then the trap was sprung and could not be unsprung and my teeth could not find my tongue to chop it off. Every fucking word she'd said for years that I'd let fester and curdle and rise and bloom within my wounded mouth were bit instead. Elysa dear they found her on her back my dear and when she said she'd fell in love Elysa dear they lashed her for lies my dear and dear oh dear how he fell upon her countless times Elysa dear and changed his mind about his love for her oh dear when they caught him dear and how he wished to live instead of love my dear in this hateful world Elysa dear where love is a possession and a prison and a fucking obligation dear instead of what it is a gift Elysa dear and so my dear stop speaking of him like you fucking own him dear Elysa dear because he is not yours Elysa dear he is his own a man my dear Byrn is his own and whomever he may give his gift my dear of love to dear and on and on and on and on I go about all the things we never say like how poor Oliver was bruised upon his back at the race in the pool and then again upon his cheek at Christmas feast and how we know they're everywhere and every time and how we know his father hates him for his frailty and failure to live up to his expectations of being a man and how she never told me what her father did to her and how we're all pretending always pretending because we're so afraid of our parents because our parents are so afraid of the guardians because the guardians are so afraid of High Father because High Father is so afraid of such a cruel and hateful god. And then. And then the words are gone. And they are struck upon her. And I cannot undo the horror in her eyes with any I am sorry. So she is gone from me. And I can only think of everything I didn't say. Of sweetest Harley, learning young, because he had to. Getting the worst of it young. Because he had to. How he might even believe it still. How his bruises may not heal beneath his skin. How they think we forget and how we want to. How poor Elysa wanted to. And so I am the devil then. In the dark of my room I put my candles on my desk and light them one by one. I make myself a devil with my makeups and my paints and my hates for myself. Black around my eyes. Black upon my mouth. Reds upon my cheeks. Whites like fresh bones that I scratch and smear like chaos. And I make myself the devil that I am so I can see the horror I have wrought with words. I bare my teeth like fangs to scare myself here in my room. I hiss the way the devil does and growl like the ghouls in hell and drag my nails along my face to scare myself here in my room. But all I do is cry. I make myself a demon in the dark and try to find her in the mirror. But she is just a girl. A girl with soft tears. A girl with a hate. A hate that I hold for them. For making me hate myself.

Harley

from his journal

He's engaged now. He [11]

---

[11] The original entry ends here. The beginning redactions appear to be his own.

Alexandra Walker

Seraphina

from her journal

We sleep with a mighty serpent, tucked tight upon his noble chest, warm between his wings and burning breath. He showers us with jewels he grew from fields up in the sky. He nurses us with godly laughter for our meals like mana from his secret heaven. His slaughter comes. We see it in the distance. The golden knight who sneaks into our orchard where we rest. The clatter of her armor keeps us up at night. The stench of her breath makes us ill by midday. And how proud she is, by his side, our mighty dragon Byrn, severing his head with an axe, parading his murder with trembling hands drenched in his perfect golden blood, dripping it everywhere, staining the cathedral rug. We knew. Like the tickle in our throats. Her conquest would end in victory. And we would have to clap. And I would have to hold sweet Harley's hand to tie him to this world. He would have ran without me. There in the church, just after the softest morning prayer, they brought them out, like winners of some prize, cattle for some sacrifice. We'd stood there once. Like all the giddy beasts poor Noah labored to keep dry. We're only good for slaughter. We're only young meat, grown to grow more meat. God devours all of us eventually. And how we smile when we're chosen. How poor Elysa's cheeks must ache tonight. Her, the conquering hero, the golden knight, slayer of the mighty Byrn. High Father prays and thanks the salivating god for such a blessed match. The prosperity of our small kingdom so secured, as it always is, every fucking time we get engaged. Hundreds of heads lower in thanks to the howling god, save three. The lovers and their bleeding Byrn. I want to keep him between my empty knuckles, right where he fits. I want to read him the list of names we would offer him. I want to hum and lull his head to sleep upon my lap. But the prayer is short, and so I only nod. For Harley has looked away. His eyes dripping confessions if he doesn't. And Byrn's eyes whisper his despair across the holy room. And then the heads are risen. The cheers. The smiles. And Byrn smiles with them. His clever smile. His smile that he taught himself so long ago. His smile he must smile when his hand rests in the hand of his betrothed. His future wife. His very future. Resting in her perfect little butcher hand. And how their hungry god must lick such slippery teeth.

Harley

from his journal

I made a wish that we could live on earth. The earth that we destroyed. Or God did, I'm still not sure. I dreamed of our life in gas masks and lead houses and new limbs and the meat of mutant things we have to hunt when my crops don't get enough sunlight.

It woke me up before everyone else. I tried to fall asleep to dream of it again, but it never works that way, does it? So I left my bed and my room and the quarters and I walked and walked and walked and I just wanted to feel small. It's so hard to feel small beneath the earth. But they made the pool so big and the ceiling of that room so tall and the glass wall so thick. It isn't even glass, I guess.

But it was dark beyond the glass still. The sun doesn't rise through the smoke, not really. But if you're lucky you can tell it's there. It's brighter by a little in the frosted gray of the glass.

I wanted to watch the brightness before the evening lights switched to days. I wanted to know it was out there in a world where we might find some place to be. I waited for it, alone in the emptiness.

And it came. And I knew then that we could find a way. I knew then that we would ask to leave, and if they said no we would do it anyway. And it wouldn't matter if we died, melting, choking on gamma rays. We'd be there. We'd be together.

And then my shadow found me. He moved slowly and strangely, and at first he wasn't much but dark and thin against the brighter gray. I thought he was me, the glow of the pool making my shadow odd against the glass. But he was free of me. He was outside the glass.

And I was so scared at first. I thought I was in trouble, one of our guardians outside had caught me out of bed at night. But they don't walk along the walls. They stand in towers and at the gates and maybe farther, at the fence. But never here. And so I was scared again because I had never seen a thing outside the glass, outside the world, outside of paradise.

I was afraid it was a beast, or a demon, or some horror. But then he was closer to the glass, and he was only two legs and two arms and one head just as I was. I did not move, and neither did he. We just stood there for a while, staring. But then he waved at me. And I waved back.

And I think he put his hand on the glass and patted it or hit it. It made the softest noise. It smudged the glass with whatever mud he had on him. I thought it was mud. I think he was hurt now. Oh God, I think he was hurt. I think that's why he was there. I think he was hurt and he needed me. He needed help.

He made a sound, like a voice, but I couldn't hear him. I tried to tell him but he couldn't hear me either. I think he was yelling. He was hitting the glass and yelling, and it sounded so quiet.

He waved again, big, fast strokes. I didn't understand at first. He moved along the glass and I followed him and he waved again. I think he wanted me away from him because then he did something. He stood strangely and then there were snaps. They startled me. They were little snaps and there were spots on the glass. And he kept doing it. Little snaps and more little spots. I think he was trying to break the glass now. I should have helped him. I didn't know how.

But then the lights outside got bright, so bright, like real lights. And they flashed and there was the wail of the siren outside. It was so quiet. And he hit the glass and he yelled and then he ran. I ran with him, along the glass, and I was saying something to him, but I don't know what it was now. I wanted to help him. But then there were more snaps, a lot of them.

And he fell. And I just watched. And he didn't move. And then more shadows came and I knew they were the guardians and I knew that they had killed him. And I just left him. I ran away, and I hid in my room. Like a useless child, crying over how useless they are.

And I know now that there is no house. There is no place. There is no life above. There's only this. There's only here. Only us, here. Trapped.

Seraphina

from her journal

Thieves have come for our sacrosanct. Their spears are long and their smiles are dizzy. We will lock ourselves inside of it and paint the walls with gasoline. We'll burn the temple to the ground before they even reach the door. It's hard to steal such fragrant lands when we have swallowed them. Our happy bodies burn inside the holy chrysalis and dance our swirling ashes into such tall forevers. One laugh, one cry, one memory. A love before your muddy boots may tread upon our flower bed. All gone into infinity. So drink our fallen hair if you must. Sleep between our smudges and our stains. Nest inside the pretty dust we left for you. Leave the faucet running and sing your shitty songs for all I care because it is nothing to the wind and rain and sky which we've become. The very gods we've learned ourselves to be we have no need of yours. And so what use are priests to those whose very lips shall be the blessing? What good are words from dead boy books when ours shall live upon our breaths? Or fathers, or mothers, or gathered believers if we are witnessed by the very night itself? Swimming in the music of our tender moans and making shelter from the presence of our promise. We are unfathomable. We are love. And you may walk into our house but you will never live in it. Camp as long as you wish, paint over the kitchen sink and pretend you're in the pictures on the wall. You will only ever be theater for husks and clatter. Asleep beside his cold and sticky bones. So marry him. Marry him in front of everyone you possibly can. Because he will be married already. He will be married to Harley. He will be married to me. He will be married. Tonight. Our wedding is tonight.

Harley

from his journal

I am getting married tonight. In secret, and in our secret way, it is only for us and held by us. I am marrying my loves tonight. Seraphina readies the cathedral for our secret ceremony as I write, alone in my room. It's important, she says, for us to be apart before.

We will be married in our hearts and that is all that will ever matter and they can never take it away from us. It's not Elysa's fault. She was forced upon him, upon us, by the pressures of God's paradise. I wish that I could tell her, that we did not have to oblige her, and play along. She's like a child telling us her doll is real, and we just have to nod along and pat her head.

So we will make our wedding real instead, for us, before we die pretending we are anything else. But I might die before them anyway, waiting here, in agony. Every little noise I hear makes me shiver. It is late, and everyone has gone to bed so long ago, and I can hear my heart racing, anticipating every moment inside of me. Not in fear, not in being caught, but in the torture of wanting them. The silence in the air surrounding me is death. The absence of their skin and fat and breaths and spit and little hairs that go unseen. I miss the strength of his hands, the music of her voice, the comfort of the three of us together as it was always meant to be.

Yet I was just with them only moments ago, in the secret sanctuary, where we agreed to meet well after midnight. It was them already there, and then me, and they were worried I wouldn't show because of how late I was, but I was so afraid to be caught out of bed then. To be followed. To be found out.

But then they soothed me in the way only they can do. By smiling at me, and kissing my cheek, and telling me, "Well, Santa saw," because he always sees, that omniscient deity of the old world, "but we will leave him early milk as penance for our sins," and so I laugh, and we begin our ritual.

She made it up, I think. But all things are made up, she says. So this was holy. Because we made it so.

We undid every button and buckle and bow from each other. Never undressing ourselves, only each other. Taking every stitch we were not born with away, until we were only us, the way God stitched us at the start. And we locked Cornelius' door of course and climbed into his bath. The one he took his life in. She said it was important to give this life to him.

We ran the water warm with our bodies in it. His blood was gone, she said, and we would give them none. We bathed one another, with slow and patient strokes. Our wet skin shining, their touches so soft and certain. And not a single kiss. Poor, impatient Byrn tried, and she pulled away with her wicked smile pinched tight, shaking her head, and telling him when we are married we may kiss.

And once we were clean, we dried each other off, and brushed each other's hair. And when he was sat on the bed, with our fingers in his hair, he cried. He asked how we could marry him when we didn't know the worst thing about him.

So Sera hid us under the covers, and in the dark, sitting in our nakedness, we made our spirits naked too. "Tell me your worst secret," she said. And he did. And it was awful. And we didn't care at all. We loved him for it. We loved the worst thing about him. Because we had to. And then we offered ours. Perhaps to break the spell, or test its strength. I think it only made us greater than we were before. First, Seraphina. Her dark and frightful things. We kept them for her in our hearts. Then me. My wretched, tragic things. My hand in theirs, my burning cheek on theirs, my secret laid with theirs. We went around in turns until there was no more. Like we had eaten all of them and found them so unfilling.

She told us everything that made us great and good and beautiful. And the emptiness of secrets shoveled out was filled with care and charity. Each of us feeding the other with all the love we saw in us. Interrupting each other, all talking at once, never ending, giggling, smiling, touching, telling, so much to tell, so many reasons why, until we only said "I know, I know, I know" because we'd said it all and knew it all and loved it all.

And then at last we left the sheets, and dressed each other in our favorite clothes, the ones we brought so neatly folded. No pinching suits or itching gowns. The soft things that billow. The old T-shirt my grandfather slept in, a giant, wide and loose upon my narrow shoulders. The denim shorts that used to be pants before they tore at the knees, which I was forbidden to wear in public.

His tank top he wears when he exercises, the sweatpants his brother used to own, now dyed a little pink from some washing accident so long ago. Also forbidden.

And her in the long fur coat her mother used to wear, the silver pants Cornelius kept hidden, some relic from a play in space. No bra, no shoes. No shoes for any of us, thank you, only toes.

These are the things that gods wear, she says.

And our faces brushed with makeup then. The soft tickle of her brush upon my cheek, my eye, my forehead. Soft colors. Soft strokes. Until we're beautiful. More beautiful than before. Than I knew we could be. Here are my eyes. Here is my nose. These are my cheeks. And his. And hers. She shows us how and lets us help. And smiles at our [12]

---

[12] An abrupt ending in the original text, presumably when Seraphina arrived at his door.

Seraphina

from her journal

Tell me your secrets, love, and I will tell you mine. Feed me from your
fingers, love, and I will feed you from mine. Share your goodness with me,
love, and I will give you mine and more and everything I find in this
creaky, wretched world. I'll light the candles while you wait, and bless each
one with wishes that I made for us. And lose count after a million. Little
fires in the sky we never get to see. I will bring them to your room for you.
My love, my love, if you will only hold my hands, and promise me. And so
they promised me. In the quiet of the witching hour, no demons are awake
but us. In the glimmer of the great cathedral. Built for gods, so why not us?
We're made of magic after all. Of spooky thoughts and sweetie-pie words
and touches that linger and smells that cuddle the insides of skulls. We're
years alive and years to go and loves to stay and come and stir and fall
away like sheets in dead men's rooms. I wish for birds to sing to us, they
sing inside my soul, anytime I find you in a crowd. Smile while you talk to
him, forever if we must, I'd cast a spell to make it so, if only I knew any.
But all I know is this. I promise you. Both. To love you as long as you love
me. In life. In death. And even after that. Whatever we may find. I'll love
you there. I promise you. We stand upon the dais before the pews we've
filled with silence and ghosts and evening secrecy. We stand beneath the
glowing Jesus in the window, blowing him kisses, knowing he means well
when he weeps. How hungry the world became while he was napping in his
heaven. How we will never fear their gnashing teeth. We are three funny
things in wedding gowns which only gods could wear. Like the knot of an
ankle. The twist in a navel. We were always meant to be. Odd apart, perfect
together. Contradictory and confusing like waters we spilled and could not
separate. We filled each other's gaps and found the shelter cozier than
home. We made it home instead. We made it a promise. To and for and
before one another. We promised. Forever, we said. Forever, and even after
that. And locked it with a kiss at once and sealed it with the wedding bed
we made from the very gowns we wore. Right there upon the holy ground,
made holy so by us. And consecrated oils brought. Stolen from the
cupboard in the kitchen. Poured into mother's bowls. Held aloft like
baptism. Washing our loneliness. Like ancient fire rights. The death the
death the death of dancing by ourselves. The hair, the flesh, the wedding
gowns. The mess we made, with more to spare, and slick between our toes.
The desperate emptiness we ache to kill, and be fulfilled. To be the dazzle
on our skin, the wet shimmer in the fire light like sacrifice. To be the
sacrificed. No hesitation. A game for virgin lusts. Only the giggle and smile
of jovial love. Perhaps the hesitation. A little only. Before the bite. The long
and gasping bite. And hands. And hands. And hands. Like some myth from

the deep. Tangling until I cannot find my own. Which hand is this? This hand is his or is it mine or his or maybe it is not a hand? His tongue perhaps, or the hairs from his head, slick and trailing like he wished to make me art. And someone's nails along my thighs, or does this thigh belong to him? Or was it always mine? The thigh he grew and gave to me, to kiss and stroke. To leave him memories in gentle bruises, like secret sheets of music, for songs of breathy moans we sing to him. Beloved and beloved. Show me where you keep your shame and I will keep it in my mouth. You will dissolve like sugar cubes and I will show you where my flowers grow. Fold yourself into my hand so I may slide my fingers there. The little strokes and taunting circles you have come to know of me. And then the earth which bore your tender heart has beckoned you come home. The gentle pull and wrap of legs. How good we've been. The open mouth and lifted chin. How nice it is to ask and nicer still to know. The gaze of tingling colors. The slip of oily touch. The shock of sweetness new. The little nod. The yes. The more. The more. The more. The kissing him while you keep going. The lay right here and grab me there. And how we've known it all but love what we've forsaken. The favorite hurt. The spill of hurt into heal and please and please and please again. The eager agony of playfulness. Give me yours while his is there inside of me. Tumble off slide between and roll within and wait and move and now higher now lower now wider now deeper now less no wait no wait please more okay again and on and on. The dance of holding and filling and rubbing and sighing. The face you make when he's in you. It's beautiful. It's my favorite face you make. It tickles deep between my brain. This mutual surrender. The sweet smell. Until we've died and born ourselves anew only to die again. And then again. Until we've given all of us and smeared our dreams into reality. Growing up like wildflowers and swirling altogether. Asleep atop the fragrance of our wedding bed. Clutching. Kissing in our sleep. Wishing we could hide within our dreams. Wishing. Until we wake up. And watch the dream crumble through our fingers yet again. As dreams are known to do in hell. Though I am known to love them still.

Harley

from his journal

Nothing good ever lasts. My hands are shaking, and they will not stop. Please, God, don't let this be the end. I'm so afraid to even write what happened. We have been found out, I know it. We were too bold last night.

We were married in our hearts last night. And it was beautiful. And we made love in the cathedral. And it was something we should not have done. It was all so beautiful, and now I feel fooled by love, and I hate that, and I hate everything. I'm so, so confused.

We fell asleep. We had sex. We had sex because we are married. And we fell asleep. It's only in our hearts but it is real because it is only ever in your heart. And we fell asleep. We fell asleep together. It was inside the church. My God. It was all so beautiful.

I promise, please, we will never do it there again.

Of course we were found out. He sent someone. God sent someone. An angel, maybe. I hope it was an angel, to scare us into wisdom.

We fell asleep, and then I heard a noise. It was a door closing. The way they do when you let them swing shut. It shut and it startled me. I thought someone came in but there was no one, I looked and it was closed, and maybe I heard footsteps. No, I did, I did, I did. I can't pretend I didn't. Someone came in while we were naked and asleep, there in the church, right there on the dais. Someone saw. Someone saw us, and they ran.

I didn't follow after them. I was too afraid. I woke Byrn and Sera and I told them someone came in and they dressed and we blew out the candles and we ran back to our rooms. She said it was fine. She said it was going to be okay.

I don't believe her though.

Seraphina

*written in the margins of Lamentations Chapter 1,
torn from a Bible, and stored in her journal*

I sneak into the freezing room where eyes don't live. I scream and scream and thrash about and laugh about how this same girl used to live in days before. How her same body might have moved alone before the mirror in some dead man's sanctuary. Songs no one may hear. Songs long dead. Songs she moved into her very flesh so she might move alone. How she might dance before herself and for herself because she loved it all. Because she was a god. And now. And now. How they have made her meat inside a freezer. Wailing. Because everything will be fine, she said. And now. Their eyes are gauzy cloths with poisoned blades just beneath. So many eyes. So many holes for eyes to live in. To walk kindly there upon the ice which I had lain for them. While I watch from far below the way they pass my secrets by. Eyes that tread so softly there upon the girl which I had built for them. A girl who was a frozen lake. The one who said her amens, her pleases, her thank yous. And moved in the footprints of fathers only. So fucking clever she used to be. And now. And now. Eyes growing gills and scales and tails so they may swim at night into our wedding bed. They are the eyes that turn. The eyes that smile. Undressing me. That say good morning and god bless you. Eyes which linger and say nothing. Eyes that quickly look away. The eyes of girls, the eyes of boys, in class, in church, and lunch and all the corners in between. And maybe, darling, they have always looked at me like so. And I have never known the eyes that know, that tell, that whisper everything we've done which they have seen. And maybe, darling, I will never know whose eyes they are. If they are eyes at all. Or hands. Or hands to hold an axe above my head.

Harley

from his journal

I want to tell my father. I want to confess it all. I want to beg for mercy. I want to be spared. I want to end it all. I want to be free of this. It is torture, God, and I am sorry. I want to make them see that we are not criminals. I want to make them know that we are good, and love, we are love, and kindness, and we are good. ██████████████

And none of it will matter. I know this. ████████████████

██████

I can't do this, God.

I want to know who knows. I want to know so I can look at them and say, something, I don't know, something. I don't want to read their little notes on bathroom stalls.

"Be careful," as though it were some kindness, some charity, some friendly warning in good will. Her name, first and last, Seraphina Caldwell, but they spelled it wrong. And then terrible names. Jezebel. Whore of Babylon. Delilah. None of them are true. And then our names. Harley Valton. Byrn Chamberley, and his had a question mark. And then they wrote "Who else?" Like a list. Like we were supposed victims, or disciples, or something.

I wanted to scratch it off, or cover it up, but I had nothing. I wanted to go back with a pen but I couldn't go back. I can't go anywhere. I don't know what to do. Please, help me.

Seraphina

from her journal

Sometimes I wish I could have seen the bombs fall. Like stars raining down. I wish I could have felt my skin and hair become the dust that chokes the sky. I wish I could have known what our last thoughts would be. Each other maybe. Fucking and kissing and tasting one another's lips and skin and fear and love. Knotting our knuckles together. Watching fire from the window we left open. Breathing it in. Breathing him in, building oceans within oceans, cradling him within my nose, cradling him within my flesh, watching him washing the memories of anything else. The same then. Our bombs fall so slowly here. Our bombs look like secrets people will not share with us. Yet here they fall and fall and fall the same. Like funny fairy things when our pretty eyes are turned away. Watching while the whole world falls within the reflection of each other's eyes. We'll never fucking learn, I guess. Alone in my bedroom. A gentle knock. The way so many scenes began. And there the ocean stands, still and desperate, gulping for the wind. Byrn, the fool, standing in my doorway, where anyone may see. I am a candle in my hand, waiting for the burning wax to drip between my fingers so. He says hello, the way a lover does when they wish to be anything else. I say hello, the way a lover does who means to pour the burning wax. And Byrn, in all his radiance, in a voice intended not to wake a fly, is meant to be with his betrothed. She is not here, Byrn Chamberley. He knows. He can't, he says. Not what, but just. He can't. And I am two words only, the way a whisper is atop a mountain, waiting. Two words. I know. And nothing else. Only eyes, the way we've done a hundred times. I never look away. My feet so softly carry me, so slowly backward to my room, deeper, deeper, deeper still. The way Elysa never would. The hesitation of his lungs. The invitation of my door. Left open. Here. The open door he shuts, like death following sickness, he follows me. So sweetly, so carefully, like tippy toes, he steps into my bedroom. The one he shouldn't be inside. The one my mother knows, and knows she may find me in at any time. But Byrn, my Byrn, he is the god beheaded, and I am his ambrosia, his salve and his anointment. I am the wetness of his thirsty lips. I am the tender gasp he drinks. I am the girl in his hands, the tongue in his mouth. We spread the earnest quiet like a sheet for us to eat upon. No locks to bother with in any case. Quickly dear, while we're alone and still alive. While everyone makes us whispers in their mouths. Sweet spectacles of sin for the ears of our friends. Lift me like a precious peace and press me down upon my vanity. The one my mother's mother gave to me. And with your fingers inside my dress, take only what you need from me. Hurry, sweet. Pull them down only so far as you will need. Let them stretch between my open knees. Let them hang there from my ankle. Let your body find mine, the way our spirits will in death. Find me, and find yourself within me. Find yourself forgetting everything this wretched world would do to you. Wear me the way mountains wear trees. Worry the way bombs worry. Let the vanity knock upon the wall. Let my moans slip between your fingers on my lips. Let them open up the door and see what we've become. And let yourself die, here with me. Spill it all inside of me. And see if we can live long enough to care.

Harley

from his journal

My journal has been returned to me by the council of Purity.

I'm not sure how to continue, or if I even should.

My father has not spoken to me. He has not even looked at me since.

They've taken Seraphina away. We don't know where she is.

I haven't seen Byrn since the preliminary trial.

They won't let us attend class. My father won't let me attend church service either.

I don't know what happens now.

I want to write it down, so I can remember it the way it was exactly.

After final bell I went to Cornelius' room. I'd wanted to be safe. I'd wanted my journal. It was in the drawer, next to his, in the secret room.

I'd thought I walked into the wrong room at first. I thought I'd been confused, under all the stress. I thought I had made some mistake and walked into some common room. But I didn't.

Elysa was there, sitting in a chair, in Cornelius' room. She didn't say anything to me. She just looked at me, and then at the wardrobe.

And the wardrobe was open. And the secret door at the back was open too. And in the secret room I saw my father. And in my father's hands I saw my journal, open too.

I didn't move. And no one said anything. I felt bare. I couldn't feel myself. It was the last time he looked at me. He stepped out, and turned me around, and gripped me by the back of my neck, and walked me out of the room. And no one said a word.

Harley

from his journal

I'm not sure what to do with this anymore. Everything I had written was accounted for during the preliminary trial, and will be used in my prosecution. It feels strange now, like I shouldn't journal in it any longer. I wonder if they'll check it now. If I write how sorry I am, if someone will read it and use it in my defense, and keep me from punishment.

It's death, of course, what they aim to give us in the end. Pending rehabilitation, technically, I suppose. But I don't know what to expect with rehabilitation, if it's conversion, if I need it, if it'll work. I don't know. I've never been pending for trial before. Maybe they'll find us pure again. And we'll get to be friends at least. Or alive, at least. Maybe.

It isn't adultery, technically. Someone would need to be legally wed. Maybe that's not so bad. They told us a list of crimes we were accused of. It wasn't adultery so maybe it won't be death. It was unchastity, and sexual perversion, and uncleanliness, and other things I can't remember. I should find those out. It wasn't death for Cornelius. Not with his trial, I mean.

The councils said they would confer with each other, and with God, before our testimonials. This is good, because God knows my heart, so He will tell them.

Perhaps Seraphina is okay. That's why there's three trials. Preliminary trial, precautionary treatment, testimony trial, initial punishments, then our final spiritual trial, and final sentencing. It is good this way. They provide so many opportunities for us to repent and prove our purity.

Her journal was damning, they said. We were so scared. She told us everything would be alright. She told us we would be together. The men of Guardianship had to pull her away from us. That must look damning as well. But we will be okay. She has most likely been taken to a precautionary treatment, wherever that is, and whatever it may consist of. I am sure it is good. She will be good.

I should have learned about trials when I was shadowing father. ████████████████████

Seraphina will be okay, and we will see her again soon. She is one of them. She is an intern with the Council of Purity. They know her. And she is smart. It will be okay. It will be good, because we are good.

Harley

from his journal

They locked me in my room today. I don't know why. They came and put a lock on my door. I never left, I was good, I obeyed my isolation. I've stayed in my room, stripped bare to walls and a mattress and my journal and my Bible and the meals they bring me on the tray with the steak knives, even when there isn't any steak.

I wonder if father wants me to kill myself.

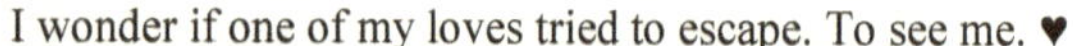

I wonder if one of my loves tried to escape. To see me. ♥

Harley

from his journal

They're worse than I remember. It's been a long time since he punished me so seriously. Maybe they really are worse than I remember. Now that I'm older, maybe he has to hit harder. I'd forgotten this side of him. It's strange now, how familiar it is. The change of his voice, the sound of my skin. I'd forgotten all about the cold little shake in my bones. It all came back so easily. Never speak, it makes it worse. Never move, it makes it worse. Only flinch when he threatens. Only cry when he's gone. So on and so on.

It was a relief, in a way, to hear him speak to me. It was good to exist again. Even then. His words of disappointment and disgust. How weak, how fortunate. How his father would have been worse. How he would never be cruel like his father. I am fortunate, to only get the rod, and not the plank or whip. Some strange justice, I suppose.

And I wonder. Would I, too, be kind like father is? Would my children find themselves so fortunate, as well? Or thankful, even, for God's loving bruises, on skin their lovers would have kissed so gently? So grateful, I wonder, if they would look at God the same.

Harley

from his journal

I saw him today. They took me to the infirmary for a checkup. Make sure I was healthy enough to stand trial and be executed, I guess. When it was done, and I was going back to my room, I realized I forgot my Bible. I had brought it with me. I don't know why. Maybe to show them I was still one of them.

After I went back to get it, and was returning to my room again, I saw him. He looked sick in a way. Pale, with dark bags under his eyes. I didn't mean to, but I cried. I was so shocked I couldn't think of anything to say, except, "Hey." And I just kept saying it. Hey. Hey. Hey.

He said my name. He said we will be okay. And I could only say, "Yeah."

He was going to the infirmary too. And because we weren't meant to cross paths, they ushered us away as quick as they could.

I would have said so much more if I had known. I would have said so much more so long ago. I would have learned to draw, I would have drawn a hundred portraits so I wouldn't forget. I would have held him more. I would have pressed my nose to his neck and breathed him in so I could remember what his smell was. I would have loved him so much more.

I don't care if they read this. I love him. And Seraphina, fuck, where is she? Why couldn't I have seen her too? God, I would have asked her everything. I would have asked her every thought she ever had so I could hear her voice and remember it like my own. I would have never let go, I would have kept my hands on her always so she knew how she was part of me. So her skin could be as familiar as my own. I would have never stopped myself from kissing her, I would have given her everything I had.

I would have let them know how much my life belonged to them. I would have cherished them so much more if I could have only known it's all we would get.

And I promise I won't touch them again if that's all that's wrong with it. If I can just see them again. If can just feel them fill a room again, and breathe their air again. God, please. Please. Give me a tongue that can turn hearts. Give me words in the trial. Let me show them that our love is good. Our love is yours. Please.

Seraphina

from her journal

Hello again, journal. It's so good to see you. I've missed writing. I want you to know, even though things are different now, since you've been read, I don't mind at all, as I no longer have anything left to hide.

It feels so good to be free of secrets, shame, and guilt. The warmth of God's light is always so welcoming, and so bright. I feel better than ever. ☺

I love God so much. I love God so much. I love God so much. I love God so much. I love God so much. I love my family so much, and I am so sorry that I ever did anything to hurt them. I won't do it again, I promise.

I miss my bedroom, and my mother, and my father. I look forward to being reunited with them. However, I am grateful to all of the Honorable Council Leaders for intervening when they did, and providing me with this space to learn and heal and grow. I am grateful to the elders, the mentors, and the Guardians for all they do.

Here is a list of what they do: They watch over me, they protect me, they pray for me, they educate me, they rehabilitate me, they provide me with food, they provide me with clean sheets and clothes, they provide me with sanitation, they feed me when I need help, they clothe me when I need help, they wash me when I need help, they discipline me, they purify me, they destroy my sinful desires, they reconnect me with God, they read to me, they talk to me, they convert me back into a holy woman of God.

I am so fortunate, we all are, and I regret spitting on such fortune. I will not do it again, ever. I have learned the error of my ways, and I hope someday soon I will not even need to be taken to the rehabilitation room. I am so thankful for all their help, but I don't want to go back.

It was necessary, but I feel much better now, and I don't want to do it anymore.

Please, don't make me.

Anyway, I promise to visit everyone here when I leave, for birthdays and such. We're friends now, and we can even throw parties in the rehabilitation room. Ha ha, just joking, that wouldn't be a very good place for a party at all.

Well, time for prayers, so, goodbye for now. Love, Seraphina Caldwell. ♥

Harley

from his journal

Tomorrow is the trial. I feel paralyzed. I can't think of anything else. I realize now the awful possibility that I will have to see Byrn and Seraphina again. That their fates may not have been as privileged as mine because their fathers are not the High Father.

Or worse, they could be doing far better, and have already decided a life without me is to their benefit. Perhaps I am the worst offender. Perhaps I am the problem.

They would dread seeing me in either scenario. But the worst case of all would be if they were relieved, and pleased by the sight of me. My heart and my spirit would be in turmoil, and there would be nothing I could do but look away from them.

And yet still, all I want in the world is to see them. In chains, in pain, even dead, just give them to me, Lord, so I may care for them and weep over them. Let me show them that our love is yours. God, please, give me strength.

Elysa

copy of trial transcription provided by the Council of Purity,
kept by Seraphina in her journal [13]

THE EXAMINATION OF ELYSA STALWRIGHT, AGE 19, WITNESS TO THE ACCUSED ACT OF SEXUAL SIN BETWEEN BYRN CHAMBERLEY, HARLEY VALTON & SERAPHINA CALDWELL, OVERSEEN BY HIGH FATHER MALCOLM VALTON, PRESIDED BY HONORABLE LEADER OF THE COUNCIL OF PURITY FRANCIS LODDEN, PERFORMED BY HIGH JUSTICE KIAN DOUGHERTY

HIGH JUSTICE:　　Ms. Stalwright, you claim to have witnessed sexual sin, is that correct?

ELYSA:　　Yes.

HIGH JUSTICE:　　Are the participants of the sexual sin in this room today?

ELYSA:　　Yes.

HIGH JUSTICE:　　Please point them out and say their name.

　　　Elysa points to Byrn Chamberley, Harley Valton & Seraphina Caldwell

ELYSA:　　Byrn, Harley and Sera.

HIGH JUSTICE:　　What did you witness them doing?

ELYSA:　　They were lying naked together.

HIGH JUSTICE:　　How were they positioned?

ELYSA:　　I'm not sure what you mean.

HIGH JUSTICE:　　Were they just lying next to one another like rows, or were they positioned in some other way?

ELYSA:　　They were in each other's arms, and on top of each other.

HIGH JUSTICE:　　Who was on top of whom?

ELYSA:　　It was—They were kind of all—I mean, it was—

HIGH JUSTICE:　　Take your time.

ELYSA:　　I didn't understand it at first.

HIGH JUSTICE:　　It's alright, of course.

ELYSA:　　Sera was kind of on top of my, of Byrn, and Harley was holding her, like next to her, or behind her kind of.

HIGH JUSTICE:　　Were they covered at all?

ELYSA:　　No, they were naked.

HIGH JUSTICE:　　Were they asleep?

---

[13] Court procedure involved providing transcription of all examinations to the accused. Although there would have been several testimonies, Seraphina apparently only kept these select few.

ELYSA: Yes.
HIGH JUSTICE: Do you believe they had been sexually immoral in any
                  way before falling asleep?
ELYSA: Yes, I do.
HIGH JUSTICE: What gives you the impression that they were sexually
                  immoral beyond lying naked together in an intimate
                  position?
ELYSA: They were covered in something like sweat or oil, and
                  it was very late, and the room had a vulgar scent. It
                  reeked of sin.
HIGH JUSTICE: I see, and in what room did you find them in?
ELYSA: In the cathedral.
           Commotion erupts from spectators in the room
HON' LEADER: Quiet. Quiet! Order in the room, please.
HIGH JUSTICE: Where in the cathedral?
ELYSA: Right there on the dais. Right in front of the cross.
              Commotion erupts in the room again
HON' LEADER: Enough! Order!
HIGH JUSTICE: What time did you find them in the cathedral?
ELYSA: Late, I don't know, early, before morning lights.
HIGH JUSTICE: Why were you going to the cathedral when you should
                  have been in bed?
ELYSA: I'm sorry.
HIGH JUSTICE: You are not in trouble, Ms. Stalwright. Why were you
                  going to the cathedral so late in the night when you
                  should have been asleep?
ELYSA: I don't know. I couldn't sleep. I wanted to pray in the
                  cathedral and look at Jesus. I'm sorry. I was engaged
                  and he was so distant and—
HIGH JUSTICE: It's alright, it's alright. Please bring a tissue.
         A tissue is brought, High Justice provides it to Elysa
HIGH JUSTICE: Did you know he would be there?
ELYSA: No.
HIGH JUSTICE: Did you think anyone would be there?
ELYSA: No.
HIGH JUSTICE: Did you feel drawn to the cathedral by any kind of
                  sinister temptation?
ELYSA: No! No!
HIGH JUSTICE: When you witnessed them in the state you described,
                  what did you do?
ELYSA: I ran away! I ran back to my room, sir! I ran! I
                  couldn't—
        Elysa loses composure in a fit of tears

HIGH JUSTICE: Did they know you had seen them?
ELYSA: I don't think so.
HIGH JUSTICE: Did they attempt to coerce you in any way to keep their
                 secret?
ELYSA: No, I don't think they knew I saw.
HIGH JUSTICE: How would you characterize their relationship before
                 you witnessed them lying naked together?
ELYSA: They were close. I thought they were just friends.
HIGH JUSTICE: Did you ever witness them in any kind of sexual sin,
                 inappropriate intimacy, or flirtatious conversation?
          No response
HIGH JUSTICE: Would you like me to repeat the question?
ELYSA: No.
HIGH JUSTICE: Why aren't you answering the question, Ms.
                 Stalwright?
ELYSA: It's just—I mean, we were playing a game, sir.
HIGH JUSTICE: What kind of game?
ELYSA: It was Sera! I tried to stop it, but she forced me, she
                 made me look stupid.
HIGH JUSTICE: What was the nature of the game?
ELYSA: It was—We would ask questions and you had to answer
                 them. But sometimes we would ask you to do
                 something, and then ask if it made you sin in your
                 heart. I didn't like it, but I never sinned, I didn't—
HIGH JUSTICE: Slow down, please. What sort of things would you ask
                 each other to do? Can you give any examples?
ELYSA: Like, to kiss someone.
HIGH JUSTICE: Did you witness them kissing?
ELYSA: Yes. They both kissed my Byrn.
HIGH JUSTICE: Whose idea was it to play the game?
ELYSA: Sera's. She invented it.
HIGH JUSTICE: Do you think she invented it to create some kind of
                 loophole so that she could kiss Mr. Chamberley?
ELYSA: I do.
HIGH JUSTICE: Did she kiss anyone else?
ELYSA: She kissed Harley.
HIGH JUSTICE: Just the two of them, then?
ELYSA: Yes.
SERAPHINA: Liar, you liar! You lie!
          *Commotion as Honorable Leader, High Justice and Council
          Members shout for order from Seraphina as she accuses Elysa of
          willingly kissing her as well, causing Elysa to shout back and
          rousing the spectators to commotion as well until Seraphina is

removed for the remainder of Elysa's examination and Honorable Leader regains control*

HIGH JUSTICE: Alright, one last question, Ms. Stalwright. Besides witnessing them kiss during a game that Ms. Caldwell made up, did you ever witness the three of them spending a lot of time together?

ELYSA: Yes! Yes, they were always sneaking off together when they thought no one was watching, but they were always gone, and—and even during a funeral I saw them sneak away together, and they pretended like it was nothing, like she was just sad, but she doesn't get sad like that, I know her, she wanted to get away somewhere while everyone was busy so she could—so she could—

Elysa loses composure in another fit of tears

HIGH JUSTICE: Thank you, Ms. Stalwright, that is all.

Harley

copy of trial transcription provided by the Council of Purity,
kept by Seraphina in her journal

THE EXAMINATION OF HARLEY VALTON, AGE 19, ACCUSED OF THE ACT OF SEXUAL SIN BETWEEN HIMSELF, BYRN CHAMBERLEY & SERAPHINA CALDWELL, OVERSEEN BY HIGH FATHER MALCOLM VALTON, PRESIDED BY HONORABLE LEADER OF THE COUNCIL OF PURITY FRANCIS LODDEN, PERFORMED BY HIGH JUSTICE KIAN DOUGHERTY

HIGH JUSTICE:	Mr. Valton you stand accused of unchastity, sexual perversion, sexual uncleanliness, homosexuality, spiritual uncleanliness, willing temptation, and deception. Do you understand this accusation?
HARLEY:	Yes, sir.
HIGH JUSTICE:	Do you wish to alter your previous plea of Not Guilty?
HARLEY:	No, we—we did nothing wrong.
HIGH JUSTICE:	That will be left to God and His Holy Councils to decide, Mr. Valton. Did you commit unchastity with either Mr. Chamberley or Ms. Caldwell?
HARLEY:	I don't think we did, no. It wasn't, I mean—And we—
HIGH JUSTICE:	Did you commit sexual perversion with either Mr. Chamberley or Ms. Caldwell?
HARLEY:	No, we love each other.
HIGH JUSTICE:	Do you understand sexual perversion?
HARLEY:	I think so.
HIGH JUSTICE:	Did you commit sexual perversion with either Mr. Chamberley or Ms. Caldwell, whether you think you love them or not?
HARLEY:	Maybe.
HIGH JUSTICE:	Yes, or no?
HARLEY:	No, no, I don't think it was—
HIGH JUSTICE:	Did you commit sexual uncleanliness with either Mr. Chamberley or Ms. Caldwell?
HARLEY:	No.
HIGH JUSTICE:	Did you commit homosexuality with Mr. Chamberley?
HARLEY:	I mean, it was—And we love Sera, and—
HIGH JUSTICE:	Do you understand homosexuality, Mr. Valton?
HARLEY:	Yes.
HIGH JUSTICE:	Did you commit—
HARLEY:	Yes.

Commotion from the spectators in the room

HON' LEADER: Enough, that's enough. Proceed.
HIGH JUSTICE: Did you commit spiritual uncleanliness?
HARLEY: Never.
HIGH JUSTICE: Did you willingly tempt either Mr. Chamberley or Ms.
                 Caldwell?
HARLEY: No, I—I love—
HIGH JUSTICE: Did you deceive either Mr. Chamberley or Ms.
                 Caldwell in order to have sexual contact with them?
HARLEY: Never!
HIGH JUSTICE: Did you deceive your parents or anyone else in your
                 community in order to keep a secret with either Mr.
                 Chamberley or Ms. Caldwell?

            Harley speaks inaudibly

HIGH JUSTICE: Please speak up, Mr. Valton.
HARLEY: Yes.
HIGH JUSTICE: Yes, you did deceive your parents or anyone—
HARLEY: Yes! Yes. I did. I'm sorry.
HIGH JUSTICE: Mr. Valton, are you a homosexual?
HARLEY: No.
HIGH JUSTICE: You admit to committing the sin of homosexuality with
                 Mr. Chamberley, do you not?
HARLEY: Yes, but…
HIGH JUSTICE: But, what?
HARLEY: I—I mean, I like women.
HIGH JUSTICE: And Byrn Chamberley, is that correct?

            Harley nods in the affirmative

HIGH JUSTICE: And you understand that Mr. Chamberley is male, do
                 you not?
HARLEY: I do.
HIGH JUSTICE: Were you coerced by Mr. Chamberley into acts of
                 homosexuality?
HARLEY: No, never, never.
HIGH JUSTICE: You willingly committed acts of homosexuality—
HARLEY: Yes, but I'm not that, I mean, I—It's different, it's—I
                 don't know how to explain it, can you be both at once?

            Commotion from the spectators

HON' LEADER: Order!
HIGH JUSTICE: Mr. Valton if you do not understand the sin of
                 homosexuality—
HARLEY: Whatever, yes, whatever I am, I don't know, fine, sure.
                 I'm not evil.
HIGH JUSTICE: Did you perform penetrative sex using your genitals
                 and the anus or rectum of Mr. Chamberley?

   No response
HIGH JUSTICE: Do you understand the question?
   Harley speaks unintelligibly
HIGH JUSTICE: Excuse me?
HARLEY: We were married.
   *Commotion from everyone in the room, including Honorable
   Leader, High Justice and Council Members*
HIGH JUSTICE: When were you married?
HARLEY: The night we were found, that's why we were in the
      cathedral.
   Commotion from spectators and Honorable Leader
HON' LEADER: Go on.
HIGH JUSTICE: Who married you?
HARLEY: We did.
HIGH JUSTICE: Please elaborate.
HARLEY: We married ourselves to each other.
HIGH JUSTICE: No one ordained by the church officiated the
      ceremony?
HARLEY: Well, we ordained ourselves—
HIGH JUSTICE: Mr. Valton, if you have anything unrelated you would
      like to say, please save it for the closing trial, you'll be
      able to make any arguments you see fit then. This trial
      is for the facts, do you understand?
HARLEY: Yes. I'm sorry. It's just that it isn't what you think.
HIGH JUSTICE: Please answer the questions honestly.
HARLEY: I will. I am!
HIGH JUSTICE: Did you perform penetrative sex using your genitals
      and the anus or rectum of Mr. Chamberley?
HARLEY: Yes.
HIGH JUSTICE: Did Mr. Chamberley perform penetrative sex using his
      genitals and the anus or rectum of yourself?
HARLEY: He did, but it—
HIGH JUSTICE: Did you perform oral sex on the genitals of Mr.
      Chamberley?
   Harley nods in the affirmative
HIGH JUSTICE: Did Mr. Chamberley perform oral sex on the genitals of
      yourself?
   Harley nods in the affirmative
HIGH JUSTICE: Did you touch with your hands or any other part of your
      body the genitals of Mr. Chamberley in a sexual
      manner intended to arouse or bring sexual pleasure of
      any kind?
   Harley cries

HIGH JUSTICE: Please answer yes or no.
HARLEY: Yes.
HIGH JUSTICE: Did Mr. Chamberley touch with his hands or any
                  other—
HARLEY: He did, yes. We both did! And we kissed! And we held
                  hands!
HIGH JUSTICE: Mr. Valton—
HARLEY: And we made each other laugh, and feel safe and good,
                  because we love each other, why aren't you asking me
                  that?

    *Commotion from spectators, as well as Honorable Leader and
High Justice attempting to keep Harley composed and on track
with answering the questions*

HARLEY: What else? Do you want to know if I smelled his hair? I
                  did! And I held him, and I massaged his feet, and I
                  watched him touch himself, you've read our journals, is
                  that all on your list? He was beautiful, and it was good,
                  and God loves us, because our love is His love.

    *Unintelligible commotion from everyone until Honorable
Leader regains control*

HON' LEADER: This is becoming a spectacle, and if you children
                  cannot compose yourselves and follow the order of this
                  proceeding you will be taken away and punished until
                  you can learn how to respectfully behave, is that
                  understood?

    *Harley regains composure from crying and nods in the
affirmative*

HON' LEADER: Finish, and please finish quickly.
HIGH JUSTICE: Um, was Ms. Caldwell present during the sexual
                  encounters?
HARLEY: Yes.
HIGH JUSTICE: Every time?
HARLEY: Basically, yeah.
HIGH JUSTICE: Did she participate in all of the sexual acts previously
                  asked and—that you have admitted to?
HARLEY: Yes.
HIGH JUSTICE: Was it willing, or did you coerce her?
HARLEY: She loves us both.
HON' LEADER: Young man…
HARLEY: She was willing.
HIGH JUSTICE: Whose idea was it to do the sexual acts, both in the
                  beginning and then each time after?
HARLEY: No one's, everyone's, I don't know.

HIGH JUSTICE: Ms. Caldwell invented the game, "Angels or Demons,"
                  did she invent other games to create loopholes that
                  made you feel you could do these sexual acts?
HARLEY: No.
HIGH JUSTICE: In her own journal she writes that she invented
                  Corporeal Studies Two, did she not tell you that she
                  was playing this supposed game to facilitate sexual
                  perversion?
HARLEY: We were all doing it together.
HIGH JUSTICE: Did she, or anyone else pressure you?
HARLEY: No.
HIGH JUSTICE: When you discovered the hidden room filled with
                  forbidden items in Mr. Clarke's old quarters did any of
                  you try to alert any elders or leaders?
HARLEY: No.
HIGH JUSTICE: Did you lie in an attempt to keep your sinning a secret?
HARLEY: I did.
HIGH JUSTICE: Besides Ms. Caldwell and Mr. Chamberley, did anyone
                  else participate in your sinfulness whether sexual or—
HARLEY: No. No one.
HIGH JUSTICE: During "Prosperity Night" as Ms. Caldwell named it,
                  who else participated, and specifically who participated
                  in the game of "Angels or Demons?"
        No response
HIGH JUSTICE: Mr. Valton?
HARLEY: I can't remember.
HIGH JUSTICE: Are you lying?
        No response
HIGH JUSTICE: Please keep in mind that your sins will be weighed in
                  the final trial.
HARLEY: I can't remember.
HIGH JUSTICE: You write that Gabriella was present and Erik took part
                  in the game. Can you confirm if these are Gabriella
                  Anderson and Erik Delorsia?
HARLEY: They didn't do anything wrong.
HIGH JUSTICE: Do you wish to refute or clarify whether or not there
                  were any inaccuracies in the testimonies from your
                  parents, peers and community members?
HARLEY: I know h/He loves us. I know it.
HIGH JUSTICE: Please answer the question: Do you wish to refute or
                  clarify anything?
        Harley shakes his head in the negative
HIGH JUSTICE: No further questions.

Byrn

*copy of trial transcription provided by the Council of Purity,
kept by Seraphina in her journal*

THE EXAMINATION OF BYRN CHAMBERLEY, AGE 20, ACCUSED OF THE ACT OF SEXUAL SIN BETWEEN HIMSELF, HARLEY VALTON & SERAPHINA CALDWELL, OVERSEEN BY HIGH FATHER MALCOLM VALTON, PRESIDED BY HONORABLE LEADER OF THE COUNCIL OF PURITY FRANCIS LODDEN, PERFORMED BY HIGH JUSTICE KIAN DOUGHERTY

HIGH JUSTICE: Mr. Chamberley, you stand accused of unchastity, sexual perversion, sexual uncleanliness, homosexuality, spiritual uncleanliness, willing temptation, and deception. Do you understand this accusation?

BYRN: Yes, I do.

HIGH JUSTICE: Do you wish to alter your previous plea of Not Guilty?

BYRN: No, I do not.

HIGH JUSTICE: Did you commit unchastity with either Mr. Valton or Ms. Caldwell?

BYRN: As you would understand it, yes.

HIGH JUSTICE: And please clarify how you believe I understand it.

BYRN: We were sexually intimate without being legally wed by an ordained member of our church.

HIGH JUSTICE: Thank you for clarifying. Did you commit sexual perversion with either Mr. Valton or Ms. Caldwell?

BYRN: As you would perceive it.

HIGH JUSTICE: Please answer, yes or no.

BYRN: You would likely… think it perverse, yes.

HIGH JUSTICE: Thank you. Did you commit sexual uncleanliness with either Mr. Valton or Ms. Caldwell?

BYRN: I don't understand the question.

HIGH JUSTICE: Which part?

BYRN: Uncleanliness.

HIGH JUSTICE: Were you ever sexually unclean?

BYRN: Do you have any examples?

HIGH JUSTICE: Sex with multiple partners, the profuse and unnecessary exchange of bodily fluids, sex during a woman's menstrual period, sex without bathing before and after.

Byrn laughs

HIGH JUSTICE: Is this a joke to you?

BYRN: No, sir.

HIGH JUSTICE: Were you ever sexually unclean?

    Byrn laughs, or cries, or both, it is unclear

HON' LEADER: Answer the question or you will be duly punished, Mr. Chamberley.

BYRN: I'm sorry, your Honor.

    Byrn composes himself with a deep breath

BYRN: Yes.

HIGH JUSTICE: Did you commit homosexuality with Mr. Valton?

    Byrn laughs

BYRN: Yes.

HIGH JUSTICE: Do you find this examination amusing, Mr. Chamberley?

BYRN: No, I do not, sir. No.

HIGH JUSTICE: Did you commit spiritual uncleanliness?

BYRN: Is that different from sexual uncleanliness?

HIGH JUSTICE: Are you getting smart with me?

BYRN: No, I don't understand the question, and it is very important to me that I answer honestly.

HIGH JUSTICE: Did you willingly submit to the temptation of sin, whether it be spiritual, mental, physical, or social, when you knew that it was wrong to do so?

BYRN: Oh.

    Silence

HIGH JUSTICE: Mr. Chamberley—

BYRN: I'm thinking.

HIGH JUSTICE: You've had ample time to reflect before the examination, answer the question.

BYRN: No. Because it wasn't. It was—It—Why do you all make us do the Blood of Christ? That's—I mean that's when it really—

HIGH JUSTICE: Please only answer the questions as they are given to you. Did you willingly tempt either Mr. Valton or Ms. Caldwell?

BYRN: No. It just happened.

HIGH JUSTICE: Did you seek them out with the intention of being a source of temptation for them?

BYRN: No, I just said—

HIGH JUSTICE: Did you deceive either Mr. Valton or Ms. Caldwell in order to have sexual contact with them?

BYRN: No, it was all—

HIGH JUSTICE: Did you deceive your parents or anyone else in your community in order to keep a secret with either Mr. Valton or Ms. Caldwell?

BYRN: Only because you made me.

HIGH JUSTICE: Excuse me?
BYRN: It would not have been like that if you would have just
                  let us—
HIGH JUSTICE: That's enough, save any arguments for the final trial.
BYRN: It's your fault!
HIGH JUSTICE: Your actions are the fault of your own self, Mr.
                  Chamberley, not mine. Now, are you a homosexual?
BYRN: If that's what you want it to be, sure.
HIGH JUSTICE: Did you perform penetrative sex using your genitals
                  and the anus or rectum of Mr. Valton?
        No response
HIGH JUSTICE: Mr.—
BYRN: Yes!
HIGH JUSTICE: Did Mr. Valton perform penetrative sex using his
                  genitals and the anus or rectum of yourself?
BYRN: He sure did.
HIGH JUSTICE: Did you perform oral sex on the genitals of Mr. Valton?
BYRN: Uh-huh.
HIGH JUSTICE: Yes or no, please.
BYRN: Yep.
HIGH JUSTICE: Did Mr. Valton perform oral sex on the genitals of
                  yourself?
BYRN: Yeah, and it was really fucking good too.
        *Commotion from the spectators in the room, Honorable Leader
        instructs the Guardians to remove Byrn for punishment and to
        resume the examination after*

THE RESUMPTION OF THE EXAMINATION OF BYRN
CHAMBERLEY, AGE 20, STILL ACCUSED THE SAME, PRESIDED
AND PERFORMED WITHOUT SUBSTITUTIONS

HIGH JUSTICE: We will pick up where we left off with the questions,
                  do you understand?
BYRN: Yes.
HIGH JUSTICE: Did you touch with your hands or any other part of your
                  body the genitals of Mr. Valton in a sexual manner
                  intended to arouse or bring sexual pleasure of any kind?
BYRN: Yes.
HIGH JUSTICE: Did Mr. Valton touch with his hands or any other part
                  of his body the genitals of yourself in a sexual manner
                  intended to arouse or bring sexual pleasure of any kind?
BYRN: Yes.
HIGH JUSTICE: Did you caress, rub, massage, hold, or otherwise touch

	Mr. Valton's body in a manner that was intentionally intimate?
BYRN:	Yes.
HIGH JUSTICE:	Did Mr. Valton caress, rub, massage, hold, or otherwise touch your body in a manner that was intentionally intimate?
BYRN:	Yes.
HIGH JUSTICE:	Did you kiss Mr. Valton on the mouth in a sensual, sexual, or romantic manner?
BYRN:	Yes.
HIGH JUSTICE:	Did Mr. Valton kiss you on the mouth in a sensual, sexual, or romantic manner?
BYRN:	Yes.
HIGH JUSTICE:	Did you perform penetrative sex with your genitals and the genitals of Ms. Caldwell?
BYRN:	Yes.
HIGH JUSTICE:	Did you perform penetrative sex with your genitals and the anus or rectum of Ms. Caldwell?

No response, Byrn appears deep in thought

HIGH JUSTICE:	Can you not recall?
BYRN:	No, I don't suppose we did.
HIGH JUSTICE:	Did you perform—
BYRN:	But we did other stuff with her butt.
HIGH JUSTICE:	Please elaborate on what you mean by that.
BYRN:	Fingers and mouths.

Commotion from the spectators

HON' LEADER:	Settle down, settle down. Quiet!
HIGH JUSTICE:	Thank you for your candor, Mr. Chamberley. Did you perform oral sex on the genitals of Ms. Caldwell?
BYRN:	Yes.
HIGH JUSTICE:	Did Ms. Caldwell perform oral sex on the genitals of yourself?
BYRN:	Yes.
HIGH JUSTICE:	Did—
BYRN:	My anus as well.

Commotion from spectators again

HON' LEADER:	I will dismiss all of you if you cannot respect this examination! Quiet!
HIGH JUSTICE:	Thank you for your honesty again, Mr. Chamberley. Did you touch with your hands or any other part of your body the genitals or breasts of Ms. Caldwell in a sexual manner intended to arouse or bring sexual pleasure of any kind?

BYRN: Yes.
HIGH JUSTICE: Did Ms. Caldwell touch with her hands, breasts, or any
                  other part of her body the genitals of yourself in a
                  sexual manner intended to arouse or bring sexual
                  pleasure of any kind?
BYRN: Yes, and my anus, don't forget my—
HIGH JUSTICE: Thank you, that's enough, we'll presume your anus was
                  involved as well.
BYRN: Thank you.
HIGH JUSTICE: Did you caress, rub, massage, hold, or otherwise touch
                  Ms.—
BYRN: Yes.
HIGH JUSTICE: Did Ms. Caldwell caress, rub—
BYRN: Yes. Yes, it's yes to everything, the kissing the
                  touching, all of it, both of us, all of us, we were in…
                  Um, I mean, yes.
HIGH JUSTICE: Very well. Whose idea was it to do the sexual acts, both
                  in the—
BYRN: Mine. It was my idea.
        *Commotion from spectators in the room as well as Harley and
        Seraphina who shout at Byrn to stop and claim that it is untrue
        thus causing Honorable Leader, High Justice and Council Leaders
        to enter the commotion with shouts while Byrn claims it was all
        his fault and his idea until Honorable Leader regains control of
        the room and a long silence takes place while High Justice writes
        and organizes papers until he clears his throat*
HIGH JUSTICE: When Mr. Valton and Ms. Caldwell presented to you
                  the hidden room filled with forbidden items in Mr.
                  Clarke's old quarters did any of you try to alert any
                  elders or leaders?
BYRN: No.
HIGH JUSTICE: Did you lie in an attempt to keep your sinning a secret?
BYRN: Yes.
HIGH JUSTICE: Besides Ms. Caldwell and Mr. Valton, did anyone else
                  participate in your sinfulness whether sexual or
                  deceit—He's—He's bleeding. Can we—Can someone?
        A tissue is brought to Byrn to stop the bleeding
BYRN: Sorry.
HIGH JUSTICE: Did anyone else participate in your sinfulness whether
                  sexual or deceitful?
BYRN: No.
        Byrn groans in what appears to be pain
HIGH JUSTICE: Alright, alright. We'll forgo the rest of the questions

	regarding Prosperity Night during the examination and ask him at another date and time.
BYRN:	It's really coming out.
HIGH JUSTICE:	Do you wish to refute or clarify whether or not there were any inaccuracies in the testimonies from your parents, peers and community members?
BYRN:	Um, yeah. I didn't win all those matches, just most of them.
HIGH JUSTICE:	Okay then. No further questions. Take him, please, before he gets it everywhere.

Seraphina

copy of trial transcription provided by the Council of Purity,
kept by Seraphina in her journal

THE EXAMINATION OF SERAPHINA CALDWELL, AGE 19, ACCUSED OF THE ACT OF SATANIC WITCHCRAFT, ACCUSED OF THE ACT OF SELF-IDOLATRY, ACCUSED OF THE ACT OF SEXUAL SIN BETWEEN HERSELF, HARLEY VALTON & BYRN CHAMBERLEY, OVERSEEN BY HIGH FATHER MALCOLM VALTON, PRESIDED BY HONORABLE LEADER OF THE COUNCIL OF PURITY FRANCIS LODDEN, PERFORMED BY HIGH JUSTICE KIAN DOUGHERTY

HIGH JUSTICE: Ms. Caldwell, you stand accused of witchcraft, devil worship, devil consortion, self-idolatry, violent thoughts, unchastity, sexual perversion, sexual uncleanliness, spiritual uncleanliness, willing temptation, and deception. Do you understand this accusation?

SERAPHINA: Mr. Dougherty, do you remember when you spoke to my class?

HIGH JUSTICE: You may refer to me as High Justice. Do you understand the accusation, Ms. Caldwell?

SERAPHINA: I do understand it, yes. It was a very exciting day for me, you're very good at what you do and I'm very excited to be examined by you, sir.

HIGH JUSTICE: Do you understand that flattery will in no way impact the outcome of your trial?

SERAPHINA: Oh, I didn't mean to flatter, sir, I just wanted to explain why I'm excited.

HIGH JUSTICE: You are excited to be examined for witchcraft and sexual deviancy, Ms. Caldwell?

SERPAHINA: Oh, no, just to experience your—I'm sorry, I won't say anything more on it, I apologize, sir.

HIGH JUSTICE: For the best. Now, do you wish to alter your previous plea of Not Guilty?

SERAPHINA: No I don't think so. Am I messing it up already?

HIGH JUSTICE: Are you a witch, Ms. Caldwell?

SERAPHINA: No, I'm a good woman.

HIGH JUSTICE: Have you ever practiced, or tried to practice witchcraft?

SERAPHINA: No, sir.

HIGH JUSTICE: What does witchcraft look like?

SERAPHINA: I don't know exactly.

HIGH JUSTICE: Have you ever been tempted to the dark forces of witchcraft?

SERAPHINA: No, I have not.

HIGH JUSTICE: Is it possible that you were unknowingly tempted into the practices of witchcraft?

SERAPHINA: I don't know, sir, how would I know?

HIGH JUSTICE: You've written very sinister thoughts in your journal, Ms. Caldwell, do you remember doing this?

SERAPHINA: Was that witchcraft?

HIGH JUSTICE: Have you ever seen the Devil, Ms. Caldwell?

No response

HIGH JUSTICE: Did you hear the question, Ms. Caldwell?

No response, Seraphina hangs her head, as though in shame or fear

HIGH JUSTICE: Would you like me to repeat the question?

SERAPHINA: No.

HIGH JUSTICE: Please answer the question, Ms. Caldwell. Have you ever seen the Devil?

SERAPHINA: I don't know.

HIGH JUSTICE: You don't know? How can you not know if you have or have not seen the Devil himself?

SERAPHINA: Because he comes in many forms, Mr. Dougherty.

Commotion from spectators in the room

HON' LEADER: Settle. Settle.

HIGH JUSTICE: Did the Devil ever come to you in any forms?

SERAPHINA: I don't want to say.

HIGH JUSTICE: Why not?

Seraphina whispers inaudibly

HIGH JUSTICE: What?

High Justice approaches her, she whispers again

HIGH JUSTICE: Say that again for the Council Members to hear.

Seraphina shakes her head in the negative

HIGH JUSTICE: He has no power here, Seraphina, you are safe.

SERAPHINA: He told me not to say.

Commotion erupts from everyone in the room

HON' LEADER: Please, please, you cannot disturb the examination! Go on.

HIGH JUSTICE: Seraphina, it is crucial that you tell us honestly what the Devil has said to you.

SERAPHINA: I'm afraid, Mr. Dougherty.

HIGH JUSTICE: You have nothing to fear, Ms. Caldwell, God will protect you, and we will protect you.

*Affirmative commotion from the spectators and Council

Members*
SERAPHINA: Alright.
HIGH JUSTICE: How did the Devil first come to you?
SERAPHINA: He came as a whisper first.
HIGH JUSTICE: The power you speak of in your journal, from
               Ascension Day.
SERAPHINA: Yes, I believe you are right. I didn't understand it then,
               but I do now. I've been feeling much better, you see.
HIGH JUSTICE: Good, that is good. We can save you.
SERAPHINA: I believe you.
HIGH JUSTICE: Did he come to you in any other forms?
SERAPHINA: Yes. He came in the form of a man, but he made me
               forget his form, he made me promise.
HIGH JUSTICE: What did he make you promise?
SERAPHINA: Not to tell.
HIGH JUSTICE: Why?
SERAPHINA: He said we weren't allowed, but that he would give me
               something great.
HIGH JUSTICE: What did he give you?
SERAPHINA: He gave me the pleasure, Mr. Dougherty, the pleasure,
               he made me swallow it so that it was inside of me, but I
               didn't like it, I never liked it, but it wouldn't go away.
HIGH JUSTICE: Is that why you gathered the children in secret to play
               the Devil's games?
SERAPHINA: Yes, he wanted me to tempt them. But I didn't want to,
               I am not a bad girl, Mr. Dougherty, I am a good girl of
               God the Holy Father, Mr. Dougherty.
HIGH JUSTICE: Did the Devil give you any other instructions?
SERAPHINA: Yes.
HIGH JUSTICE: What were they?
          Seraphina hangs her head and shakes her head in the negative
HIGH JUSTICE: Ms. Caldwell the only path to redemption and freedom
               from the Devil and his sins is through confession and
               forgiveness, now what were the Devil's instructions?
SERAPHINA: He wanted Byrn and Harley, too.
HARLEY: No! No! She's lying! She loves us! There's no way!
          *Commotion from High Justice and Honorable Leader attempting
          to silence Harley, commotion as well from Council Members and
          spectators as Harley continues to cry out, begging her to tell them
          it wasn't the Devil, until he sobs unintelligibly and is escorted out
          by force*
HIGH JUSTICE: The High Father's son, and a well-liked, well-respected
               young man. Did you lead them into temptation then?

SERAPHINA: I did.

HIGH JUSTICE: Did the Devil give you anything else, besides what you refer to as the pleasure?

SERAPHINA: Yes, he gave me a vision.

HIGH JUSTICE: What was in the vision?

SERAPHINA: I was on a throne, and I was covered in—in—Oh, no. No, no, no. Not again, not—

HIGH JUSTICE: What is it? Are you alright?

Seraphina continues breathing heavily and stammering

SERAPHINA: It's happening again.

Seraphina moans and groans vulgar noises of pain or ecstasy, she appears to lose control of herself, wailing and moaning as though in a sexual state, lolling her head backwards and sideways, panting and either convulsing or gyrating, or both, she puts her head on the wood and runs her tongue along the railing, moaning still, commotion erupts from everyone, shouting in shock and fear, attempting to return her to a respectable state, until she has calmed and pants heavily in exhaustion

HIGH JUSTICE: Seraphina Caldwell, explain yourself.

SERPHAINA: Please, please, please, forgive me, I cannot control it, it is him, it is the pleasure, please, please, please, help me, sir.

HIGH JUSTICE: We will help you. Has the Devil possessed you in this manner before?

Seraphina nods her head in the affirmative

HIGH JUSTICE: Are you well enough to continue?

Seraphina nods her head in the affirmative

HIGH JUSTICE: Did you commit unchastity with either Mr. Valton or Mr. Chamberley?

Seraphina nods her head in the affirmative

HIGH JUSTICE: Did you commit sexual perversion with either Mr. Valton or Mr. Chamberley?

Seraphina nods her head in the affirmative

HIGH JUSTICE: Did you commit sexual uncleanliness with either Mr. Valton or Mr. Chamberley?

Seraphina nods her head in the affirmative

HIGH JUSTICE: Did you commit spiritual uncleanliness?

Seraphina cries

SERAPHINA: He told me it would be okay.

SPECTATOR: Let her have a break.

Commotion from spectators in agreement

HON' LEADER: That's enough, that's enough! Ms. Caldwell? Ms. Caldwell, do you require a break from the examination?

    Seraphina shakes her head in the negative, Honorable Leader nods to High Justice

HIGH JUSTICE: Did you willingly tempt either Mr. Valton or Mr. Chamberley?

SERAPHINA: He made me do it.

HIGH JUSTICE: Did you deceive either Mr. Valton or Mr. Chamberley in order to have sexual contact with them?

    Seraphina nods in the affirmative

HIGH JUSTICE: Did you deceive your parents or anyone else in your community in order to keep a secret with either Mr. Valton or Mr. Chamberley?

    Seraphina cries and nods in the affirmative

HIGH JUSTICE: We're nearly finished. Are you sure you don't need a break?

    Seraphina nods in the affirmative, a tissue is brought to her

HIGH JUSTICE: Did you invite and allow Mr. Valton to perform penetrative sex on your genitals with his genitals?

    Seraphina nods in the affirmative

HIGH JUSTICE: Did you invite and allow Mr. Chamberley to perform penetrative sex on your genitals with his genitals?

    Seraphina nods in the affirmative

HIGH JUSTICE: Did you have penetrative sex with them individually or together?

SERAPHINA: Both. I would have sex with one of them sometimes, and sometimes it would be both at once, but it was never both of them inside my vagina at once, it was too tight, so I would take the other one's penis in my hand or my mouth, or he would just lie and watch, and touch us, or himself, or sometimes he would enter the other one's mouth or anus.

HIGH JUSTICE: Did Mr. Valton perform penetrative sex using his genitals and the anus or rectum of yourself?

SERAPHINA: No, neither of them did, but I think I wanted to try it, but when it would happen, they would just enter my vagina, or my mouth. I think it's because it was wet already, sir.

HIGH JUSTICE: Did you perform oral sex on the genitals of—of them both then?

SERAPHINA: I did. And I would use my hands, like it says in the book.

HIGH JUSTICE: What book?

SERAPHINA: The book of the Devil. I was to take their cock in my mouth, I mean their penis, and suck on it with my lips, and rub it in and out on my wet tongue—

       Seraphina sticks her tongue out to show High Justice

SERAPHINA: And then with my hand I would stroke the length of it, gripping and rubbing, and I would moan while I did so, whether it was in my mouth or not, I would go—

       Seraphina demonstrates a sexual moan

SERAPHINA: Like that.

HIGH JUSTICE: Ms. Caldwell, is it your intention to tempt me?

SERAPHINA: Do you find me tempting, Mr. Dougherty?

HIGH JUSTICE: Is it the Devil that I am speaking to in this moment? Is he speaking through you?

SERAPHINA: Do you wish to speak with the Devil, Mr. Dougherty?

      Hushed commotion goes uninterrupted from the spectators, High Justice clears his throat and reviews his papers

HIGH JUSTICE: Did Mr. Valton perform oral sex on the genitals of yourself?

SERAPHINA: He did.

HIGH JUSTICE: Did Mr. Chamberley?

SERAPHINA: Yes.

HIGH JUSTICE: Did you, um, did you kiss them? Mr. Valton and Mr. Chamberley?

SERAPHINA: Yes, on their mouths, and elsewhere.

HIGH JUSTICE: It was part of the temptation?

SERAPHINA: It was.

HIGH JUSTICE: Whose idea was it to do the sexual acts, both in the beginning and then each time after?

SERAPHINA: Mine. Or the Devil's, I couldn't tell.

HIGH JUSTICE: When you discovered the hidden room did you tell anyone?

SERAPHINA: No.

HIGH JUSTICE: Did you lie in an attempt to keep your sinning a secret?

SERAPHINA: Yes.

HIGH JUSTICE: Besides Mr. Valton and Mr. Chamberley, did anyone else participate in your sinfulness whether sexual or deceitful?

SERAPHINA: Not yet.

      Commotion from spectators and Honorable Leader attempting to silence them

HIGH JUSTICE: Will you tell us who else you tempted, whether in a game or otherwise?

SERAPHINA: He always makes me forget. I'm sorry, Mr. Dougherty.

HIGH JUSTICE: Do you wish to refute or clarify whether or not there were any inaccuracies in the testimonies from your parents, peers and community members?

SERAPHINA: I kissed Elysa Stalwright. I think she might have liked it.

Commotion erupts from the room, Honorable Leader attempts to shout them down as High Justice concludes his questioning, and Seraphina is escorted out

Harley

from his journal

They wouldn't listen to me. No one will listen to me. Why did she say that? Why did he? What is happening? God, what is happening? I don't understand. It isn't true. Why is everything like this? Why did she say that? I don't believe it. I can't. I can't. I won't. It wasn't true. It can't be. It can't be. It just can't. It can't be the devil. We were God's love. We are. Why is everything like this?

Why?
Why?
Why?
Why?
Why?
Why? Please, God, help us.

Seraphina

from her journal

Here is a list of things our God is:
>Good.
>Powerful.
>Right.
>Unbeatable.
>Wise.
>Loving.
>Merciful.
>Fair.
>Just.
>Kind.
>Everywhere.
>Smart.
>Good.

Ha ha I have written good twice. But He is. He is good. Even his punishments are good, because his punishments rectify our crimes, and I want to be rectified.

Our punishments before final trial will be fair and just and kind. They will hurt and that is the feeling of God's light cleansing our bodies of sin.

It would not hurt if we were not stained by the filth of our sins.

The Devil is inside me. It will hurt to tear his claws from inside of me. It is right to hurt.

I love when God hurts me. Because it is good hurt. ♥

Harley

from his journal

Mr. Brecard says it's good to journal about my progress. Preliminary punishments have begun. I can't remember if it was a couple days or a week ago. It's hard to tell sometimes. They don't let me have my journal. Only when they read my old entries to me during sessions.

I've found them very helpful.

I think I am doing well. I have noticed a change. I am quiet, and listen well, and answer honestly. It hurts sometimes. But I have been good at it. I am quiet.

I did not cry so much today. This is good. I hope it is working. And I will be able to plead our case in the final trial of the spirit, and it will make sense to everyone, that even though we were wrong, ██████████ ██████ we still meant to be good.

Or maybe we didn't. Maybe it really was the Devil. Mr. Brecard says it was. I don't know though, because I did not ever see the Devil. I only saw my friends, whom I meant to love.

Mr. Brecard says it's time to finish. I hope it's only prayers.

I always hope it's only prayers.

But I think he's getting out the machine again. I haven't gotten good at the machine. But I will. I will be better. I know it.

Seraphina

from her journal

Be quiet, Satan. I don't have to listen to you. Love, Seraphina.

134

from her journal

Be quiet, Satan. I don't have to listen to you. Love, Seraphina.

Harley

from his journal

I used to think my love for Byrn Chamberley was romantic love.
I was wrong to think my love for Byrn Chamberley was romantic love.
I now understand with clarity that my love for Byrn Chamberley is only
brotherly love that all men of God share.
The devil tricked me into perverting my love for Byrn Chamberley.

I used to think my love for Seraphina Caldwell involved sexual love.
I was wrong to think my love for Seraphina Caldwell involved sexual love.
I now understand with clarity that my love for Seraphina Caldwell is only
romantic love.
The devil tricked me into perverting my love for Seraphina Caldwell.

I used to think that the love of three friends could involve sexual love.
I was wrong to think the love of three friends could involve sexual love.
I now understand with clarity that sexual love can only exist between one
man and his wife.
The devil tricked me into perverting my love for my friends.

I used to think my love for Byrn Chamberley was romantic love.
I was wrong to think my love for Byrn Chamberley was romantic love.
I now understand with clarity that my love for Byrn Chamberley is only
brotherly love that all men of God share.
The devil tricked me into perverting my love for Byrn Chamberley.

I used to think my love for Seraphina Caldwell involved sexual love.
I was wrong to think my love for Seraphina Caldwell involved sexual love.
I now understand with clarity that my love for Seraphina Caldwell is only
romantic love.
The devil tricked me into perverting my love for Seraphina Caldwell.

I used to think that the love of three friends could involve sexual love.
I was wrong to think the love of three friends could involve sexual love.
I now understand with clarity that sexual love can only exist between one
man and his wife.
The devil tricked me into perverting my love for my friends.

I used to think my love for Byrn Chamberley was romantic love.
I was wrong to think my love for Byrn Chamberley was romantic love.
I now understand with clarity that my love for Byrn Chamberley is only
brotherly love that all men of God share.
The devil tricked me into perverting my love for Byrn Chamberley.

I used to think my love for Seraphina Caldwell involved sexual love.
I was wrong to think my love for Seraphina Caldwell involved sexual love.
I now understand with clarity that my love for Seraphina Caldwell is only romantic love.
The devil tricked me into perverting my love for Seraphina Caldwell.

I used to think that the love of three friends could involve sexual love.
I was wrong to think the love of three friends could involve sexual love.
I now understand with clarity that sexual love can only exist between one man and his wife.
The devil tricked me into perverting my love for my friends.

I used to think my love for Byrn Chamberley was romantic love.
I was wrong to think my love for Byrn Chamberley was romantic love.
I now understand with clarity that my love for Byrn Chamberley is only brotherly love that all men of God share.
The devil tricked me into perverting my love for Byrn Chamberley.

I used to think my love for Seraphina Caldwell involved sexual love.
I was wrong to think my love for Seraphina Caldwell involved sexual love.
I now understand with clarity that my love for Seraphina Caldwell is only romantic love.
The devil tricked me into perverting my love for Seraphina Caldwell.

I used to think that the love of three friends could involve sexual love.
I was wrong to think the love of three friends could involve sexual love.
I now understand with clarity that sexual love can only exist between one man and his wife.
The devil tricked me into perverting my love for my friends.

I used to think my love for Byrn Chamberley was romantic love.
I was wrong to think my love for Byrn Chamberley was romantic love.
I now understand with clarity that my love for Byrn Chamberley is only brotherly love that all men of God share.
The devil tricked me into perverting my love for Byrn Chamberley.

I used to think my love for Seraphina Caldwell involved sexual love.
I was wrong to think my love for Seraphina Caldwell involved sexual love.
I now understand with clarity that my love for Seraphina Caldwell is only romantic love.
The devil tricked me into perverting my love for Seraphina Caldwell.

I used to think that the love of three friends could involve sexual love.
I was wrong to think the love of three friends could involve sexual love.
I now understand with clarity that sexual love can only exist between one

man and his wife.
The devil tricked me into perverting my love for my friends.

I used to think my love for Byrn Chamberley was romantic love.
I was wrong to think my love for Byrn Chamberley was romantic love.
I now understand with clarity that my love for Byrn Chamberley is only brotherly love that all men of God share.
The devil tricked me into perverting my love for Byrn Chamberley.

I used to think my love for Seraphina Caldwell involved sexual love.
I was wrong to think my love for Seraphina Caldwell involved sexual love.
I now understand with clarity that my love for Seraphina Caldwell is only romantic love.
The devil tricked me into perverting my love for Seraphina Caldwell.

I used to think that the love of three friends could involve sexual love.
I was wrong to think that love of three friends could involve sexual love.
I now understand with clarity that sexual love can only exist between one man and his wife.
The devil tricked me into perverting my love for my friends.

I used to think my love for Byrn Chamberley was romantic love.
I was wrong to think my love for Byrn Chamberley was romantic love.
I now understand with clarity that my love for Byrn Chamberley is only brotherly love that all men of God share.
The devil tricked me into perverting my love for Byrn Chamberley.

I used to think my love for Seraphina Caldwell involved sexual love.
I was wrong to think my love for Seraphina Caldwell involved sexual love.
I now understand with clarity that my love for Seraphina Caldwell is only romantic love.
The devil tricked me into perverting my love for Seraphina Caldwell.

I used to think the love of three friends could involve sexual love.
I was wrong to think the love of three friends could involve sexual love.
I now understand with clarity that sexual love can only exist between one man and his wife.
The devil tricked me into perverting my love for my friends.

I used to think my love for Byrn Chamberley was romantic love.
I was wrong to think my love for Byrn Chamberley was romantic love.
I now understand with clarity that my love for Byrn Chamberley is only brotherly love that all men of God share.
The devil tricked me into perverting my love for Byrn Chamberley.

I used to think my love for Seraphina Caldwell involved sexual love.
I was wrong to think my love for Seraphina Caldwell involved sexual love.
I now understand with clarity that my love for Seraphina Caldwell is only romantic love.
The devil tricked me into perverting my love for Seraphina Caldwell.

I used to think that the love of three friends could involve sexual love.
I was wrong to think the love of three friends could involve sexual love.
I now understand with clarity that sexual love can only exist between one man and his wife.
The devil tricked me into perverting my love for my friends.

I used to think my love for Byrn Chamberley was romantic love.
I was wrong to think my love for Byrn Chamberley was romantic love.
I now understand with clarity that my love for Byrn Chamberley is only brotherly love that all men of God share.
The devil tricked me into perverting my love for Byrn Chamberley.

I used to think my love for Seraphina Caldwell involved sexual love.
I was wrong to think my love for Seraphina Caldwell involved sexual love.
I now understand with clarity that my love for Seraphina Caldwell is only romantic love.
The devil tricked me into perverting my love for Seraphina Caldwell.

I used to think that the love of three friends could involve sexual love.
I was wrong to think the love of three friends could involve sexual love.
I now understand with clarity that sexual love can only exist between one man and his wife.
The devil tricked me into perverting my love for my friends.

Mr. Brecard says that is enough.

Seraphina

from her journal

Once upon a time, there was a beautiful princess in a beautiful kingdom, very far away. It was a kingdom built out of stars, and God loved it very much, and He loved the beautiful princess very much as well.

On the princess's birthday, a beautiful man came to visit her. He wore a mask to hide his face, and the mask was very beautiful as well. During her birthday party, he gave her a gift. The gift was a magical mirror that would change the princess's face into funny shapes.

The princess loved the gift, and laughed and laughed and laughed and laughed and laughed and laughed and everyone started to notice that she was laughing too much. When they asked her why, she told them it was the mirror, but no one thought the mirror was funny.

When she asked them why, they told her that the mirror wasn't showing her fake shapes, but was actually changing her bones and hair. She did not understand that the funny things she saw were monsters, and that she was the monsters.

The king and queen and all the friends the princess had tried to make her stop looking in the mirror, but she did not listen. She broke the mirror, and stabbed everyone with the broken pieces, which was a very bad thing to do.

Everyone was mad at the princess, and she needed to be helped. She had been tricked by the man in the mask. So they put her in a tower where he could not reach her, and only visited when they needed to give her medicine.

The medicine was lots of things, because she had changed into lots of monsters. The medicine went everywhere because the mirror changed her everywhere. They even had to put the medicine on her private parts, because the mirror had made her sick there.

Even though it made her hurt, the princess knew it was good. But the medicine they gave her was not enough to fix her, so men would come into her tower at night, and give her more.

When the princess is freed, she will be healed, and she will be so thankful.

Harley

from his journal

My father and my mother visited me today. It was good.

But I made a mistake. I didn't think he would still be angry with me for the trial. He was. He didn't want to hear it. I shouldn't have. I should have known. He wouldn't look at me. Only mother spoke. I should have known.

I wanted to make him see what we meant, not what we messed up. That it was a love I had confused. That I wouldn't touch her until we were married, and that I wouldn't touch him again. I promised. I just wanted to love him the right way now. I just wanted mercy. He's my father and he's important. I just wanted him to know what we meant. To see. I just wanted to be able to love them right.

But I'm not good with words.

So he had to punish me. Because I'm stupid. Because we can't ever see each other.

Maybe he thought I meant homosexual love. I don't know.

I think I've made him hate me.

I can't live in this world.

Seraphina

from her journal

It was funny at first, when they put us in the same room, I could not help but laugh. We were all so scared to see each other without our parents watching. But God was watching, so, really, I guess I don't know why it was so weird. But it was.

Even though I was laughing they did not laugh with me. That made me sad. Nothing was the same now. Not since the truth was out.

I said I was sorry, but they kept looking around in that funny way. They looked like they were going to be sick right there on the carpet. I wondered if they heard me, so I said I was sorry again. Harley asked why I lied during the trial, but I did not lie, so I told him so.

I told him I didn't mean to lead them into temptation, and that I didn't know it was the Devil at first, but Harley did not believe me, and that made me sad.

Byrn said he wasn't supposed to be in there with us, and he was not supposed to talk to us, and that he needed to leave, but we were locked in, and I told him he was silly, because this was a test. Harley didn't understand, so I said it again, I said it was a test. He really should get smarter if he doesn't want the Devil to tempt him again.

Harley kept talking about the trial. He said he didn't understand why we both lied during the trial, that he didn't believe me, and that it was never Byrn's fault, and he didn't understand. But Byrn just told him to please stop talking to him. He was starting to cry.

When Harley went to him, I reminded him it was a test. We shouldn't touch. The Devil wanted us to touch. Harley was mad at me. He said it was all wrong. He said he wasn't going to touch us like that, he said he loved us, he wanted to feel us and comfort us. We were arguing.

He begged me. He was being pushed by the Devil, I think. He said we're alone, but I reminded him God was watching. God was always watching.

He kept asking what they did to me. He kept asking why I was different. And I kept having to tell him they helped me, that they made me better. But he wouldn't stop. He wanted to know what they did.

I did not tell him. It was private.

So he told us what they did to him. He told us everything, and I told him to hush, because that is private, but he would not stop. He went on and on, and he made Byrn cry, but I would not let him make me cry. I told him to shut up. I told him over and over again, like I tell the Devil, but it was "Shut up, Harley, shut up."

He said we didn't mean to be bad. I said none of God's children means to be bad, we just are. Then Byrn said they were good to Harley because he was the High Father's son, and that made Harley angry. Harley told us how his father punishes him extra, so Byrn told us how the Guardians and others punish him extra too. I did not say anything, but I know.

They punish him when everyone is gone at night. They press him down so they can build a hell for him to live within. So he can know why what he's done is wrong, why he is disgusting, and what a world without God's love can feel like.

Harley said they aren't allowed to do that, and that they will be punished. But Harley does not know they will not be punished. So Byrn told him this, which made Harley say that God would punish them then. And that's what made Byrn say it.

He said there is no God. He said God is evil. He said he hates God.

We did not talk after that. At least, not for a while. We just sat apart without looking.

Eventually Harley asked what we were going to do. I said we were going to tell the truth. But Byrn still wanted to take the blame. I said it wasn't his fault, and he said it wasn't mine, and I said of course, it was the Devil, and they got mad at me. They wanted me to tell them I lied, but I did not.

Harley asked what happened to us. I didn't say anything. Neither did Byrn. So Harley said he was going to beg for mercy. He said he loved us, and he was going to promise never to do it again, so long as we could just be friends. He said God loves the way we love, and we just made a mistake, and that it wouldn't happen again.

He is so silly. They will never let us speak again. I told him so, and he got upset again.

But I knew what was right and so I told those boys what was right, that the only path to redemption was confession, repentance, begging for forgiveness, and abstinence from sin. We will never be allowed to speak again, touch again, or see each other again. The only permittance we will have to be together again, ever, is if they hang us together.

I don't know why, but poor Harley looked so shocked. And shocked worse when Byrn said that it was okay to die together. He said it was better that way. But Harley just kept saying no, and trying not to cry. And Byrn didn't seem to mind. Byrn just looked at me and said, "Never again," and asked if I remembered. It must have been the Devil because I don't remember. But he said I made him promise, "Never again," so I just told him that was the wrong promise.

He seemed sad then, but I don't know why. The Devil must have broken his heart.

They would not speak then, so I reminded them, because I am

patient: Confession, repentance, forgiveness, abstinence. We must turn away from the Devil and devilish things. We must live in the light of the one true God.

Byrn looked at me for a long time, and it made me feel uncomfortable, because I was afraid he was having sinful thoughts, but I have faith he was not because he said, "Okay, Seraphina, we will do it your way." So I had to correct him, and tell him it was God's way.

I think Harley was still trying to convince himself we did nothing wrong because he was starting to say something like that, that we didn't do anything wrong, but Byrn turned to him and told him we will get to live.

At first, Harley just kept looking at Byrn and myself, but then he nodded, and that was that. I led us in a prayer, and we thanked God for the opportunity to prove ourselves, and after some time they came and took us away.

The end.

Harley

from his journal

I wish we could have been born in another time, or another place, or with different bodies. I wish we could have figured it out and done it right. But it's just a wish, and God doesn't grant wishes.

I don't know what hope there is for us. Tomorrow is the final trial. Confess our sins, demonstrate our repentance, beg for forgiveness, and abstain from sin henceforth. And then what? Live? Is that what it means to live? To bleed ourselves out in a tub one day? I'd rather live. But in another world. One I can't seem to find yet.

I just wanted them to know. To remember. Remember that my hands were good, that my skin was okay, and that there was love in this. That it wasn't all bad. It was only bad when they told us so. But nothing is the same.

I wonder if they recognize me. I cannot recognize them. A Byrn who doesn't smile. A Byrn who is afraid again, and ashamed of his fear, and would rather die than be ashamed. A Sera with no fire. A Sera blunted, who sees devils now, and desires only to submit. What of me, then, I wonder? What have I become? Someone they do not know? Someone they could not love?

I think so. And so we'll live. We'll give up, and we'll live. God give me strength to live.

Seraphina

from her journal

I remember who the Devil is.

Harley

*copy of trial transcription provided by the Council of Purity,
kept by Seraphina in her journal*

THE FINAL PLEAS OF HARLEY VALTON IN THE CASE OF SEXUAL
SIN, OVERSEEN BY HIGH FATHER MALCOLM VALTON, PRESIDED
BY HONORABLE LEADER OF THE COUNCIL OF PURITY FRANCIS
LODDEN

HARLEY:	Honorable Leader, thank you for the opportunity to plead my case before my community, my family, my friends, my respected Council Members, and most importantly, before God, the Holy Father. I would like to begin first by saying to you all that I am very sorry. I have been accused of sexual sin, which I am guilty of in the eyes of God, and the eyes of our holy law. I regret ever falling for the temptations of Satan, and straying from the holy path. The harm I have caused to myself, my family, my friends, and of course God, is painful, shameful, and embarrassing. I am eternally grateful that we were found out, so that we could be saved. I—

Harley stops reading from his paper, hesitates, and appears to fight back tears

I know now that I was confused, led astray, and never meant to pervert the love of my friend and my betrothed. I beg for your forgiveness, in your own time, as I work to undo the damage I have caused, and continue to abstain—

He hesitates again, and wipes his eyes

To abstain from further sin. I pray that you will all forgive me for my transgressions, and—and—

Harley stops reading, he appears to look at Byrn and Seraphina

I just want you to know we never meant for it to be wrong. I want you to know in my heart I meant every good thing. I want you to know that it never felt wrong when we were together. Maybe it was the Devil, like you say, but it only ever felt like God.

Commotion from the room before Honorable Leader can regain control

It did! It—I know sin! I know it as you know it! We crossed the line of the law but it was never meant to be bad. Please, understand. It came from love. It did. Do you understand? I love them!

Commotion from the room

    It's strange, but God works in ways that seem strange at first, does He not? Does He not? Please. Please! Father, please. Look at me, father. Please look at me. Please! It was always in love. Okay? I love her. I love him.

Unintelligible due to commotion from the room

    Please! God loves all of us! He loves everyone! He loves me! He does! I know it! I only meant to love like He loves! Why can't we love like God loves?

Unintelligible shouts from the room before it becomes a chant from the spectators

SPECTATORS: You're not God! You're not God! You're not God!

HON' LEADER: Enough! Enough! Quiet! Take him away. That's enough!

    Harley is removed from the stand, still pleading and crying

Byrn

*copy of trial transcription provided by the Council of Purity,
kept by Seraphina in her journal*

THE FINAL PLEAS OF BYRN CHAMBERLEY IN THE CASE OF
SEXUAL SIN, OVERSEEN BY HIGH FATHER MALCOLM VALTON,
PRESIDED BY HONORABLE LEADER OF THE COUNCIL OF PURITY
FRANCIS LODDEN

For a long while, Byrn remains silent on the stand

HON' LEADER: Mr. Chamberley, you may begin.

Byrn looks at him and nods, then looks around the room, and stares at Harley and Seraphina for a while longer

HON' LEADER: Mr. Chamberley if you do not have any final arguments please step down.

BYRN: No, I do. I do. Sorry. Um, right. Thank you all for coming to my trial. It means a lot to see you all here. I'm sorry if I ever hurt any of you. I never meant to. When we were, um, tricked by the Devil into committing sexual sin, it was wrong. I regret it. I never should have done it. I'm sorry. I never meant to hurt anyone. Please, find it in your hearts to forgive me. It won't happen again.

Byrn mumbles inaudibly

Forgetting something. Oh, I promise to never look at Harley or Seraphina again. I promise to be a good husband to Elysa, if she will still have me, and if she won't, then I... promise to be a good—Just good.

HON' LEADER: Is that all?

No response, Byrn looks at Seraphina and Harley

HON' LEADER: Mr. Chamberley?

Byrn looks away and nods

BYRN: Yeah. That's—That's all of it.

HON' LEADER: Very well then.

Byrn remains seated, staring at Seraphina and Harley

HON' LEADER: You may be dismissed, Mr. Chamberley.

BYRN: Right. Right, of course.

Byrn leaves the stand

Seraphina

*copy of trial transcription provided by the Council of Purity,
kept by Seraphina in her journal*

THE FINAL PLEAS OF SERAPHINA CALDWELL IN THE CASE OF SATANIC WITCHCRAFT, THE CASE OF SELF-IDOLATRY, AND THE CASE OF SEXUAL SIN, OVERSEEN BY HIGH FATHER MALCOLM VALTON, PRESIDED BY HONORABLE LEADER OF THE COUNCIL OF PURITY FRANCIS LODDEN

SERAPHINA: I can see him so clearly now. I promised not to say, but I can do all things through Christ who strengthens me. I see that now. I came to confess, and confess I shall. I remember who the Devil is, and was, and always will be. He came to me in the night when I thought it just a dream. But he tormented me so, and oh how he has since. He hid his face but I can see him now. He made me do it!

Seraphina points directly at Byrn, commotion erupts from the room

Byrn Chamberley tempted me! He is the wolf in sheep's clothing! He is the thief in the night! He is the Devil himself! I have seen his darkness!

Unintelligible shrieks and shouts and commotion

BYRN: No! No! No! No! No!

Seraphina faints, Byrn is apprehended and removed by the Guardians, shouting objections, Harley is held down, the Guardians force back the spectators as they attempt to chase after Byrn with great commotion

Harley

from his journal

I don't understand. I just don't understand.

It's a lie. It wasn't him. Please.

She's lied. She's betrayed us. She's going to hell. I hate her.

I can't stop. I'm going to die this way. Please, God, kill me. Kill me. I don't want to do this anymore. I'm sorry.

Byrn

*copy of final verdict provided by the Council of Purity,
found among Byrn's things*

IN THE CASE OF THE ACT OF SEXUAL SIN BETWEEN HARLEY VALTON, AGE 19, BYRN CHAMBERLEY, AGE 20, AND SERAPHINA CALDWELL, AGE 19, AFTER CAREFUL EXAMINATION CONDUCTED BY HIGH JUSTICE KIAN DOUGHERTY OF THE ACCUSED AND WITNESSES TO THE CRIMES AND CHARACTER OF THE ACCUSED, AS WELL AS FINAL PLEAS OF THE ACCUSED, INCLUDING ALL REVELATORY CONFESSION AND INFORMATION CONTAINED THEREIN, AND AFTER DELIBERATION AMONG MEN AND ENLIGHTENMENT FROM OUR HOLY GOD HIMSELF, HIGH FATHER MALCOLM VALTON, HONORABLE LEADER OF THE COUNCIL OF PURITY FRANCIS LODDEN, AND RESPECTED MEMBERS OF THE COUNCIL OF PURITY IN THIS SESSION HAVE UNANIMOUSLY FOUND THE CULPRIT OF GUILT TO BE BYRN CHAMBERLEY ALONE, HAVING LED ASTRAY THE HOLY LAMBS OF THE NEW EDEN OF GOD THE FATHER: HARLEY VALTON, SERAPHINA CALDWELL, AND ANY OTHERS YET KNOWN, WHETHER BY DIRECT OR INDIRECT POSSESSION OF THE ENEMY SATAN OR BY DIRECT OR INDIRECT ACCORDANCE WITH THE ENEMY SATAN OR AS THE ENEMY SATAN HIMSELF DISGUISED AS THE SON OF MIRIAM CHAMBERLEY AND GODRIC CHAMBERLEY, AND SHALL THEREFORE BE SENTENCED TO DEATH BY DISMEMBERMENT BEFORE A VOLUNTARY COMMUNAL WITNESS OF THE HOLY COUNCILS OF GOD AND THE HOLY PEOPLE OF NEW EDEN. IN THE CASE OF THE ACT OF SATANIC WITCHCRAFT AND IN THE CASE OF THE ACT OF SELF-IDOLATRY BY SERAPHINA CALDWELL, CONDUCTED, OVERSEEN & DELIBERATED BY THE SAME, SERAPHINA CALDWELL HAS BEEN FOUND NOT GUILTY, HAVING BEEN OVERWHELMINGLY COERCED BY THE ENEMY SATAN AS SEEN IN BYRN CHAMBERLEY, ALTHOUGH HER CRIMES EXISTED HER REPENTENCE IS SINCERE AND HER PUNISHMENT THEREFORE SHALL BE PROBATIONARY SUPERVISION BY THE COUNCIL OF PURITY WHILE BEING ALLOWED TO REMAIN BETROTHED TO HARLEY VALTON. SO SAYS HIGH FATHER MALCOLM VALTON WITH ALL AUTHORITY GRANTED BY THE HIGHEST FATHER GOD ALMIGHTY, MAY HE HAVE MERCY ON YOUR SOUL, AMEN.

Byrn

written on the back his final verdict

I thought I was loved finally.
I thought I was known finally.
Understood by them entirely and
I wasn't.
I was nothing. I was never
My loves were a lie.
Everyone hates me.
My mother is ashamed.
My father is ashamed.
My brother is ashamed.
They don't believe me.
They don't know me.
They don't even care to.
I am all alone. A freak. A creature.
How could anyone have ever loved me?
Idiot.
Of course they hated me.
I am disgusting.
I hate myself.
I was never loved.
It was all a lie. It was a prank. I am abandoned.
My loves were fake. My loves. They have abandoned me and my
Delusion. I was delusional.
Of course they think I tricked them, and forced them, and hurt them.
Because it is disgusting.
Of course I am the devil.
And of course I deserve to die.
Of course. Because after everything
All of it. I still love them.
And always will.
Seraphina Caitlyn Caldwell.
Harley Justice Valton.
I love you. Both.
With everything. Still
And always will.
I am so, so very sorry.
I never meant to hurt
I never

Harley

from his journal

It's a day for death. I don't believe any of it. How the world has changed in just one day. It seems so long ago. Ages. It was only this morning. My god his execution was this morning. And now here I sit, writing. There is blood on my page. It was real. We are here. I'm still shaking, I can't get it to stop. I don't know why I'm writing. I can't think of anything else. I can't do anything else. She's going to die. I have to put it here. There's nothing I can do. It should be here. It should be somewhere. Somewhere else. Before she dies.

It was this morning. His execution was this morning. She betrayed us, and they sentenced him to die. It was this morning. We were there in the cathedral. They wanted to do it someplace holy, someplace God could watch and approve of. It was sickening. He didn't put up a fight. He just walked on with them, with the executioner. I couldn't help it. It doesn't matter now, but I think I was thinking something different would happen, and I didn't want to cry, but I couldn't help it. And she was there too. Everyone was there to watch. Everyone was there to watch them take him apart. Or was it everyone? It seemed like so many. It mustn't have been them all. It couldn't have been. But I was there. My father was there. The councils. Guardians. Everyone who mattered.

They didn't light the candles. It was just the glow of the stained glass lights. It was dark. And it smelled so clean. It smelled so beautiful and looked so wonderful that I wanted to scream. I'm sure I did. They stood him up there, and I can't even remember what they said. They said it like it was nothing. They said it like morning announcements. Then my father asked if anyone had anything they'd like to say. And I couldn't even move. I wanted to say everything. I stood up, I remember that, but I couldn't think of anything to say. And he just kept looking at me, and smiling, Byrn was smiling. And all I could do was cry.

And no one said anything, and father left the dais where we were married. And the executioner grabbed his big axe and pushed Byrn onto his knees. He was so gentle and I wanted to scream, and at first I thought I did, but it was her. It was Seraphina.

She was standing on the pew above everyone and she was screaming for him to wait. I was so afraid. I thought she was going to make it worse. I wanted to tell her to shut up, I remember that, but I couldn't get words to come out. But he did, he did wait, the executioner lowered his axe. She said she had something to say, and they let her walk up to the dais, and they let her stand right next to Byrn. It wasn't fair. I remember I was so jealous. I wanted to stand next to him too. And yet I did not move.

And she spoke. She asked them why they were killing him. They said he was a devil. She asked them if it was because she had said so. They said it was. She asked them, "And what if I did not see the devil?" They said he must still die, for tempting us, for anything, because it was God's will, it was God's command. She said, and she said so loud, "I have looked upon the devil, and seen nothing. I have looked upon the God, and found nothing. There is only us. No command. No will. No need to kill the man, this boy. His crimes are my crimes. He only didn't think to lie. He only thought to love. You will kill this man for loving? For touching his loves the way his lovers asked?" And they said yes. And she said to them, so loud, with tears in her eyes, "Please, friends, elders, fathers, we have been hit and pulled and ripped and hurt enough by fathers in this room. We have been raped in the darkness by your neighbors for crimes you have decided were deserving of such. Crimes you have decided must exist. Do not kill this boy. Say that enough has been dealt."

And then, one by one, I watched everyone decide, at last, not to say that enough had been dealt. They let the silence speak for them. And father stood at last to say that she had lied and she had sinned and so she too must die. And everyone agreed.

"Kill her first." He said it so calmly. I thought I misheard him, because of how calmly he said it, but then the executioner stepped toward her, and he lifted his axe.

It didn't make sense to me when it happened. He was big and lifting the shiny weapon. He was above her. She was so small before him. Her arms were at her side, but then her hand was lifted too, it reached all the way from her body to his throat, and I didn't see it at first, but he had stopped. He just stood there, coughing so quietly. No, choking, he was choking on his blood. And she pulled a knife from his throat and his blood kept squirting out. I thought at first it had been there all along. But it was her. A knife, the one from our secret room, the one that hides in the handle but flicks out when you press the thing. She had stabbed the executioner and he was bleeding and then he was on his knees and everyone was gasping and she stabbed the executioner again, putting the knife into his eye.

He fell and everyone screamed, and Seraphina screamed as well. She had his blood on her. But her scream was not the same, she was yelling, she was yelling at everyone. And I was closer to her. I didn't remember moving, but I had. At some point I had leapt up from my seat and gone to her. And I could see the blood on her face and her hand. And I could hear her yelling at everyone. They were all standing, but no one went to her.

She said to them, her arms held high, the bloody knife in one hand, and an old lighter in the other, she said, "I am your God now. I have weighed your sins, and I have found you wanting." She flicked open the cap of the old metal lighter, and I knew it was the one from our secret room as well. She said to them, "I am your merciful God, and you will hear me. Choose. Stay and kill the boy. Stay and kill the sinners who love in ways that frighten you. Stay and burn. Or leave. Leave now. Forgive him. Forgive me. Forgive Harley. Forgive us and let us live." And then she did the thing that makes the fire light, and she told them, "Choose."

But no one left. They looked at her. They looked at each other. They looked confused and they muttered their disbelief. And I remember one man laughed. And I remember hearing my father's voice.

He told me to stop her. But I did not. I looked at her, and she smiled at me in that way you wouldn't know unless you knew her as I do. And so he told me to come to him. He kept telling me, over and over, "Come here, Harley, now. Get over here. Now." And I did not. I looked at him. I remembered him. And I realized a father's love should look like something else.

I stepped back, and I joined my love. And she said to them, "Please, do not do this."

But they did. Two and three at a time, they came closer. They did not leave like she asked. They closed in to kill us.

And so she dropped the lighter. And when it fell it lit a holy fire. A miracle. A flame so fast and wide it swallowed everything before us in a moment. It spread like gallons of water dumped along the floor. It ran up the walls and doors. It was so hot. And we were spared.

All around the dais we were safe. Byrn, and me, and Seraphina. The fire would not touch us. Only everyone else. And I was afraid at the horror. The councils, the leaders, the neighbors who came to watch Byrn die, all dying around us. All burning. All in a hell that Seraphina had created like some saint in a story. Fire and screaming. And I was afraid because I was relieved. I was afraid because I realized how thankful I was. How they had hurt my loves. How they had hurt me. How they were meant to be our friends and neighbors. How hungry they looked to see Byrn's body in pieces. How much they hated us before. I was afraid because I didn't want them dead, even if they wanted us to die.

And when I finally turned to Byrn and Seraphina they were in each other's arms. She was saying something that I could not hear, and she was holding him so tightly. And I knew it then that nothing she had said was true. That all of her betrayal was nothing more than a play for her. A trick to trap them here. A lie to get her revenge.

And so she was in my arms too. Both of them. And she was apologizing over and over and over and Byrn had to kiss her just to make her stop. He never stopped loving her. He told her, and I realized I didn't either. And everyone was dying. And we were going to die as well. And I was scared again. I didn't want to die, but there wasn't any way to live.

We'd been trapped as well. But I was happy I was with them.

The fire was getting closer and we had to back away, closer to the stained glass light of Jesus. I was crying, and I was laughing, and I was saying that I was happy I was with them, even at the end. But Byrn wasn't listening.

He ran to the fire. He grabbed the axe. And he returned to us, and he was looking around. And then he looked at Jesus, and he swung the axe at him. I was overwhelmed. I didn't stop him. He just kept swinging, and smashing the window into pieces, and the light fixture into pieces and then a thin little wall behind that.

And there it was. It was a dark hall. It was freedom. And he dropped the axe, and he stepped through, and he reached his hand out to us. "It's not the end," he said. It was a service hall. So engineers could fix Jesus from behind. He must have seen it on a map.

He led us down, and out a service door. And then we didn't move. And I remember I asked Seraphina why, and she said it was the only way. I think she was right. I wish she weren't.

"What do we do?" Byrn asked. And Seraphina laughed. She said she didn't know. She said she didn't get this far.

"Why don't we leave?" I asked. And I wish I hadn't. But I had wanted to leave for so long. I had wanted to be outside. I had wanted to be gone with them. Away.

And Byrn asked where, and I told him where, I told him outside. I told him above.

And he said we'll need to pack, and it sounded funny in a way, and so we laughed. Then Seraphina said we'll need to pack, and we nodded. And so we went to the quarters together, and I was so thankful there were no alarms, but now it seems wrong that there weren't. But miracles seem wrong I suppose.

And as we made our way I remember everyone we passed seemed so strange. They looked at us strangely, I mean. Yet they did not speak to us. They did not stop us. And then I could hear people yelling. And people would run past us. They were running to the fire.

We only separated to pack in our rooms. I didn't have much. I didn't know what to bring. I should have done it differently. I only grabbed this, and some clothes, and my Bible. It was fast. And we met in the hall.

We were going to the stairs. We just had to take them all the way up and go outside. But everyone was panicking now, because there was a fire in the church, and the alarms wouldn't work, and there were no sprinklers. We were so close.

But a group of people stopped us. Because we had been in the cathedral, and Byrn was supposed to be dead. I said it was a miracle. But they said it was a fire. I had known these people all my life. I had seen them all. They asked how it started and I said it was a miracle, but they wouldn't listen. "Where are you going?" they asked. "We need help."

Seraphina stepped forward then. She said we were leaving, that they were going to kill us. The people asked what we had done. Seraphina said they were corrupt and cruel, that they hurt us and were going to kill us. I said we were leaving. I said the world above is free. The people said it's only death above.

Byrn asked them to come with us. Byrn said we could be free.

But they hated us. They said we were sinners. They said we couldn't leave. They knew we started the fire. And they attacked us. All of them. There were so many, and so many more came. I had known these people before. But I was not one of them.

We had to fight them. We had to hit them, and kick them. We had to run. But they kept coming, they kept trying to grab us. They were dragging Sera by her hair, they were dragging her down the stairs and they were holding me and pulling me and I was so afraid. But Byrn was always so strong. He fought them. He punched them again and again and again. He became something else that I had not seen. He beat them until their faces were red with blood.

Then we were running again. I think Sera cut her hair. She had the knife still and I think she cut her hair with it. Her hair was shorter.

We ran up the steps and they tried to follow us and we kicked them down. We were so close. We made it all the way to the top. Our hands were on the door.

It was death outside. It was chaos outside. It was pain and fear outside. We had never been. But it was for us. It was us, together, free. I pulled the locks and I turned the wheel with them and we opened the door.

It was beautiful. It was nothing I had imagined. It was bright, and it was cool, and the air was new. It was the stones and the walls and the fence. But it was trees then. And clouds and sky. And we ran.

But it was the alarms then. It was the men of Guardianship with their guns. They were yelling. And the stones around our feet blew up like little pops. And the bangs from their guns hurt my ears and made me jump. But we ran. We were so close.

I could see the fence. I could see the gate. It was a door we could open. We were so close.

Their hands were in mine, and we were running.

And she fell. She screamed only once. She wasn't in my hand. She was on the ground.

We tried to help her up. We tried. We were so so close.

But she was so slow and she was hurt. She was bleeding. It was getting on me. It was everywhere. She wanted us to go. But we didn't. She fell and we fell with her.

And I thought we were all going to die. They were shooting still, and running to us.

But then there was more shooting. And loud noises, like old engines. There were big metal machines with wheels. They crashed through the fence. They had come from outside. And there were people. They were in jackets and masks and things. They had guns and they used them to shoot. But they didn't shoot us. They shot the Guardians, and the Guardians fell.

But they were too late. They had come for us. But Seraphina was too hurt. They carried her, and they pushed us into their machine. Their vehicle.

I held her hand. And he held her hand. And I didn't hear anything they said to me. They were talking, and they were just people. No monsters. No mutants. Just faces. Just hair. Just arms and hands. They were us, unlike anything I'd seen, but they were us.

And I wanted Seraphina to say how beautiful they were. I wanted her to see them. But she wouldn't open her eyes. She wouldn't stop bleeding. They can't stop her bleeding.

We were so close. But none of it matters now.

Seraphina

from her deathbed, transcribed by Dawn

One last confession for God's prettiest witch. I am no saint, in the end. No matter what they say, I'll never forgive myself for hurting them. They were light in darkness. They were warmth in cold nights. They were love in a hell without hope. I broke their hearts and I will find myself in hell for it. It was only ever a theater for revenge. For our freedom. Peace at the cost of tragedy. A character to hide behind, a broken girl, so weak and scared of superstitions. The only thing they ever wanted girls to be. It was the very first night. They tore me from the arms of my loves, it was like tearing my own arms away. They tortured me for being everything they never wanted. Wild. Defiant. Skeptical. Sexual. Opinionated and profound and pleasurable and thank god I didn't fuck their daughters too. Imagine. I hated them. And there was no god to punish them. So I became their god of retribution. It was that very first night, a whisper, that they would die for everything they did to us. And so I had to hurt my loves and lie and live and gather every villain in a room so I might strike upon them every fury I could carry. Because I used to be a jewel. The pride of my crop. A fucking key card, for a fucking internship, to every fucking room I'd ever want. In the night before his execution I became their devil. I became their witch. Gathering every chemical I could to craft some concoction of fire with perfumes too so I could hide its true intent. Malevolence. I worked all night. It burned my lungs and split my fingers and made me fear that I would breathe fire when it came. I scrubbed and I painted every inch of their little arena for his death. I saved a spot for us to hold each other. I never thought we would live. Better to die together than wait and die each day without them. I made it smell like sunshine and roses and clean water. I turned off the sprinklers. I cut the alarms. I timed the doors to lock. I hid Cornelius' treasures in my dress. A switchblade and a lighter. A scepter and an orb. And words that I dreamed might move their hearts. Forgiveness. They wouldn't. Their teeth were slick with a hungry drool for death. Righteous murder by holy hands. And I was only meat in the way. I killed that man with my knife. I can't unhear his sounds of fear. I can't unfeel the heat of his blood on my skin. I can't unkill any of them. I know a hell awaits me now. I only meant to be the fear they made me out to be. I burned them all. Every hungry man who meant to torture us. Every hungry eye who meant to watch with glee the body of an innocent man, the body of my love, split into pieces. Every hungry rapist whom holy men would pat on the back and kiss on the cheek. And so I wonder what hell there is for those who kill their rapists. I hope it isn't bad. Temperate at least. I would do it again. To hold my Byrn and whisper every truth and sorrow and apology that can never replace the hurt I gave to him. The angel Byrn. The boy who knew that Jesus saves. You only have to kill him first, and he will lead you out of hell. He saved us. And Harley saved us too. He brought us out. He is the best of us. He is the air. I think I'm going to miss them. I'll haunt them, I think. I think they'll like that. Until they're ready to be dead with me. I wonder if it'll be different this time. I almost died before. That day. They shot me in my chest, those fucks. It hurt so fucking much, you have no idea. I think I maybe did die actually. It scared your father. So much blood. But they saved me. Your godmother actually, did you know that? She saved us that day, and she told me not to die, and even when I did, she brought me out of it. And I lived. I woke up and I saw the dawn. For the first time in my life, I saw the sun rise. It was this hope. This life. It was every day after, it was a new thing, and I was a new thing. It's why we named you Dawn. You were everything. I'm so proud of you. Your fathers are too. You'll need to take care of them. I've been taking care of them for fucking ever, someone has to do it. Don't laugh, I mean it. Your mothers too. They seem stronger than they are. We all do. Be good, love. Be happy. Whatever it means to you. Don't ever forget how strong you are. And send your little monsters in when you're done, I'd like to see them before it gets too bad. I'm done, I think.

ACKNOWLEDGMENTS

I never thought I was the kind of girl who wrote books, let alone the strangely horny, epistolary, post-apocalyptic, dystopian, romance books. I was wrong, clearly, and I'm grateful to everyone who helped me realize it.

This story started out as one thing that I lost interest in and nearly discarded until my brilliant friend, Stanley Swindling came along and helped me fall in love with it again by offering a better way to tell it. He's a genius, and this book wouldn't be here without him.

Eric, Norm, Maya, Lori, Amber, Cliff, and Rikki were all kind enough to read this and tell me what they thought. Their warm praise and feedback helped nourish my confidence in this book, and it wouldn't be here without them.

Dr. Aaron C. Thomas was an early mentor who helped guide me through a difficult turning point in my life, and has always encouraged me to continue writing. This book wouldn't be here without him.

Sydney Rose Walker, however, made sure this book existed. She read it first, night by night, entry by entry, begging for more and telling me when Seraphina made absolutely no fucking sense. Then, she forced me to share it with people. She is the Harley to my Seraphina, and this book would simply never exist without her.

Alexandra Walker is published with Marvel comics, has had plays staged in several states, and is the recipient of the Cypress Dome editor's choice award. Having grown up in small, conservative towns as a closeted, pansexual, polyamorous trans girl with both a Wiccan and Baptist upbringing, she knows how to have a sexy little party with all the weird, sad stuff in life. Fortunately, she now lives in the lesbian part of Los Angeles with her wife and a degree in Theatre Studies.